How to Build a World

By:

Russell Nohelty

and

Claire Venus

Edited by:

Lily Luchesi

Proofread by:

Toni Cox

This is a nonfiction work. Russell Nohelty and Claire Venus do not guarantee any outcomes from following the advice in this book. We are not lawyers, accountants, or other specialized professionals. We take no responsibility for what happens if you take this advice. It's worked for us and many others we know. However, this is simply the accumulated experience of two people making their journey into the world. While we think it is very good advice, there is no guarantee it will work for you.

First Edition, October 2024

About the Authors

Russell Nohelty

Hi, I'm Russell Nohelty. I'm a USA Today bestselling author, for one. Additionally, I've helped hundreds of authors scale their mailing lists.

People generally know me as a fantasy author, comic book creator, and professional speaker, but I'm also a serial creative entrepreneur. Throughout my career, I have owned a movie production company, a photography studio, a Verizon dealership, and more.

Currently, I own Wannabe Press and co-founded Writer MBA with my business partner, Monica Leonelle. Together, we also co-founded the Future of Publishing Mastermind and co-created the Author Ecosystems.

With such wide-ranging interests and skills, I tend to think about building an author career differently from most writers, integrating lessons from every industry I've worked in to help you create a more robust and sustainable business.

I've written over 40 novels, yes, but I also write nonfiction, comics, and children's books. I have written for magazines and newspapers across the country, along with working on licensed content for many companies. I've created over a dozen courses and built countless websites. I have worked with hundreds of photography clients and traveled around the world to work on movies. I've directed television and written web series. I have produced audio dramas, narrated audiobooks, and hosted podcasts. I've spoken at conferences, educational institutions, and private companies around the world and sat on advisory boards across multiple creative industries. I have licensed books to board game companies and coffee distributors. I've had my work optioned by studios and pitched to companies like Nickelodeon and Disney. I have been repped by literary agents and managers and worked with A-list showrunners to package projects for Hollywood. I've sold my books into translation and done book signings on multiple continents. I have edited and contributed to dozens of anthologies. I've raised close to a million dollars on my creative projects throughout my career and helped hundreds of creatives build successful careers for themselves.

I've touched almost every facet of authorship and creativity and been blessed to be pretty successful with most of them. Even the ones that flamed out taught me a lot about how to build a path for other people.

Through my work with Monica, though, I've come to understand the ever-changing landscape of publishing in a way I never have before.

I've also spent hundreds of hours researching successful Substack publications to create these guides for you. Ready to become a Substack rockstar? Then, let's get into it.

A note from Russell

I've been a fan of Claire's work since I first stumbled across her in the early days of Notes. I found her work as exhaustive as I found her boundless energy endearing. Stumped by how much engagement she gets on her articles, I hired her as my engagement consultant and quickly found that being Claire was exhausting. I couldn't keep up with her enthusiasm, especially with my chronic conditions, but I love everything about her and what she's doing here. I send people to her all the time and consider her one of the top experts on building a Substack from the ground up that fills you with joy instead of weighing you down.

After Monica told me she wouldn't be available to co-write this book with me, I had a bit of a freakout moment. It didn't last long because I quickly realized I already had the perfect Substack platform expert to help me get this book over the finish line. Claire and I have been looking for a project to work on together for a while, and both of us love helping people on Substack so much that this felt like the perfect fit.

I tend to be steadfast, practical, and just a little (or a lot) overwhelming, while Claire is a constant enthusiast who will pick you up, dust you off, and get you excited to try again. It's a great combo, I think, and I adore everything she brought to this book. It's everything I thought it could be and more.

Claire Venus

Claire Venus is an Engagement Consultant and Creative. She began using Substack in April 2022 and started teaching others how to use it a year later. She lives on the Northumberland Coast in the UK with her husband, two children, and five pet chickens.

Claire's work has spanned over two decades in the Cultural and Heritage sector at home and abroad. She has won three Journal Culture Awards for her project work in dedication to creative expression. She celebrates a Substack income of over $35,000 per year and is dedicated to helping people stay creative and build publications, which are a joy to write for.

A note from Claire

Someone once said I should write a book about Substack.

It turns out someone else said the exact same thing to Russell, so we had a chat and decided we'd write it together!

That's the short and sweet story of "How to Create a World-Class Substack" came to be.

It's over 80,000 words of our individual and collective experience of the Substack platform from 2022 2024.

This book is a how-to guide.

It's also a deep dive into the bigger questions about why you might want to create a world-class Substack, how to do that work and what we do on the platform.

If you want to get to grips with what it will mean for you if you make Substack your online home, we've got you covered.

We live 5,000 miles apart, and I first discovered Russell's work through Substack Notes (Substack's built-in social media channel). It was shortly after Notes launched, and I found his take on business, author growth, and Substack to be wholly refreshing. As a Substack educator with over 300 members, I immediately wanted to partner with Russell.

He is a fantastically talented writer. More than that, he is a supporter of the working world of words and an all-round generous human. His mindset (in my opinion) is responsible for 80% of his success. The rest is down to carefully considered action and aforementioned talent.

He's utterly brilliant. Our values are very aligned, especially with the work in service to creators.

I call him the Substack Wizard. If you've spent any time reading his content or delving into his articles, you'll know why.

Russell has a unique viewpoint on why we should start and grow a Substack publication. He's savvy about how it fits and knows how best to utilize the technology to network, grow, and develop your business.

His maverick way of guiding you through a complex platform leaves you both stunned and inspired. He openly shares what has worked for him and how he strikes a balance between writing great articles in service to creatives and running multiple 6-figure businesses.

The more time I spend with Russell, the more I realize he is both ahead of the game and one of a kind. There is no one else like him, and it would be an impossibility to imitate any of his genius.

I am delighted to have worked with Russell to edit this book for you. You'll see where I've chipped in to your depth of understanding of how to build a world-class Substack.

I've simply added the words;

***

'With Sparkle...'

when I've had something to add.

***

With gratitude and so much respect for this beautiful connection.

We can't wait to watch you set your ideas in motion and see you build a world-class Substack.

Introduction

Ready? All aboard!

We are big believers in bringing an embodied self to your work. We also know you must have a way to put your work down and immerse yourself in your hobbies, the things you love and living a life.

Right here and now, we are asking you to bring attention to tuning into how you feel as well as what you think. To write from your heart as well as using the brilliance in your mind.

We've chosen an ocean analogy to introduce you to your unique place here on Substack.

Because it's relatable, it will help you imagine what it is you're about to navigate. Because visual analogies stick in our brains more than lists of information.

Ready to set sail? Great!

Ok, first, you'll need your boat.

Building your boat, the right boat at the right time for the right conditions—we've got this!

But wait...you don't know the conditions yet because you have yet to learn Substack as a platform. And there's the small matter of building a boat from scratch.

We hear you, and we're going to give you a quick, six-step Substack manual to help you get on your way.

This is your quick start guide, your A-Z of Substack, before we drill deep into the good stuff: the nuance and strategy. You can skip this part to circle back or read it and implement everything we advise—the choice is yours.

This is designed to give you an overview and get you thinking deeper about what you want and what Substack can do for you.

Let's pause and zoom out.

This is a whole new map of your creative life. It's familiar territory, but there are subtle differences to learn and lean into.

Ready to grab a notebook and pen? You'll need those and some time. We'd advise beginning a new notebook for your Substack publication. You'll need it to be sizable.

You can take notes electronically, of course, but 99% of the creative issues I mentor people on are solved with a notebook and pen. Writing and using color are the strongest hotlines we have for our creative intuition.

There's lots to learn and plenty of inspiration for ideas to generate.

Substack is a FREE-to-use platform. It makes money by charging 10% of all paid reader subscriptions and with investments. They promise this will always be the case. No ads. No algorithm between you and your readers.

If you're not sure if you want to build here on Substack, we'd say go for it.

You don't have to tell anyone yet. Perhaps that seems counter intuitive? Hear me out?

If you build it all just for you to start, your confidence will soar when you do launch.

Or if you don't like the sound of that, tell everyone who will listen and encourage them to celebrate your journey. It's really up to you.

We all create with a world of experiences behind us. Some of us are introverts, some are extroverts, and some need to build the posting and publishing muscle. For others, they come to Substack ready to set off fireworks.

Once you've built it and spent time with it, you'll be able to articulate what it is. That is the hardest part as you build your identity and a settling-in period comes.

Next, you'll work out what you want it to be and the best fit for your online work and brand.

Building your boat, Piece by piece!

First, you need to decide what Substack is going to be for you.

Do you want to start a newsletter, post essays, move an existing podcast, start a podcast, make video episodes, grow a community, share workshops and more behind the scenes of your process?

All of the above is possible.

What do YOU want?

If you can't answer that, what do you THINK you want?

To...

1. (Just) write a newsletter.
2. Write and share posts.
3. Host a podcast.
4. Share video.
5. Grow a community.
6. Grow subscribers for your newsletter here or on other platforms?
7. Transition away from algorithmically-controlled platforms?

Write one or all of these down.

Your Engine Room

Now, it's time to tend to your Substack engine. This is the place below deck just for you. It's the place of the endless settings page. You can tinker here to set things up.

Do you know those complex toys with a quick setup guide? We made you one for your Substack.

Once you are set up with your about page and you've figured out how you want to capture the attention of the folks who land there, that's really it. Everything else you'll grow into in time.

HOMEWORK: As well as setting out your stall, you want to subscribe to AND recommend some of your favorite writers/creatives to begin making connections. This is the signal to the Substack engine room across the island, sharing more about what you love, like, and want to see.

Navigating crisp, turquoise blue waters

Your ship's navigation system is built in the form of your dashboard. Here, you can find your stats, lists of subscribers, recommendations, some email filters and lots of cool statistical data. You can also send an email from here without it posting to your Substack 'website'.

If you've gone all-in with podcasts, posts, and videos, you can check what's happening with delivery rates, open rates, engagement, and more here. This is a very useful place to spend time when you're figuring out what works AND balancing that with what feels good.

Take a look at the world map and visualize all the places you want your work to be read and seen.

HOMEWORK: If you're the type of person who finds it hard to watch subscriber numbers go up and down or stagnant, we suggest bookmarking your writer dashboard rather than your stats page.

Have you got your compass ready? Which way do you want to travel, and for how long?

Your boat's steering wheel is your content calendar. Where you travel is your content pillar.

We will expand on this in a forthcoming chapter. In our opinion, you want to set a cadence that works in your week and leave time to read, engage and write. Your content pillars want to celebrate both who you are and what you do. It needs to be clear to people. Strip out anything that gets in the way of clarity.

With 1-2-1 clients who run successful businesses, we start with a seasonal cadence. That's four newsletters a year. Once we commit to this work, ideas will spill out, and that number will more than double.

HOMEWORK: decide which day of the week you are going to dedicate to Substack. Write it down, set an alarm, and make an appointment with yourself. Do what you need to do to make sure you show up. You can tinker in settings, write, read, comment, and hang out in Notes. Just promise you'll show up.

Ships run on multiple types of fuel

On planned downtime, pausing paid subs and burn out.

It's exciting to build a world-class Substack. If you're doing one or two things right, you'll be gaining subscribers most days. If you're producing excellent articles and hosting a community, it will be more. If you're actively using Notes, it will be even more than that.

An anecdote from Claire:

In April 2023, I took a holiday and kept the Substack app on my phone. I observed my nervous system. I wrote in my notebook. I mixed up my experience. I wasn't logged in on my browser, so I naturally took a break from understanding what my subscriber and paid subscriber numbers were doing.

All in all, there were pleasant surprises for me when I returned.

I'd spent some time working out some important sums while sipping coconut water on a sun lounger.

The sums showed me what it would take at my current rate of growth to get to $5k annual recurring income on Substack. I made that my goal when I returned and hit it a few months later.

In April 2024, I did the same thing: I took a break, but this time, I took the app off my phone and scheduled posts. I was so ready to untangle myself from notifications and the timepiece of being plugged in. It worked wonders for my nervous system, and I returned home to $30k GAR.

Boundaries online are vitally important. They are also something completely unique to many of us. They are something we must set and reset as we learn more about how our Substack works and how we work as we plug into it.

We have time; there is so much time. Good things are coming—write that on a post-it note on your fridge.

The internet is a hungry ghost. It's also a lifeline of sophisticated connection.

You can walk the tightrope of what you want it to be for you, and you can mix that up every day if you choose to.

You're in charge, you're driving the whole boat, remember?

A storm comes in...

Sometimes, you are knocked off-course without warning. A storm comes in, there's a power outage, and you see yourself in the pitch black of night and wonder what it's all for.

Should you pause, stop, get support?

A shoal of rainbow-colored fish swims past. A brilliantly blue dolphin. A rainbow unicorn flies on by—life is passing us by while we're behind screens. Make a life you want to put your phone down for, then circle back and write about it on your Substack!

Perhaps it's time for a pause, or perhaps you have outgrown your content and need to make a new section or space for your creativity.

A tropical parrot sits on your shoulder and whispers what you want to hear. A friend, a confidant, a set of people to turn to, a Substack educator.

Plain language, accountability, a critical friend, a mentor. Who would you like to confide in? The world is full of helpful people.

Perhaps there's some reciprocity to be found.

Sometimes you feel like you're doing ALL the things, A LOT of the right things, and doing them both together MOST of the time, but the needle is stuck.

Subs aren't coming, or if they are, they're not engaging. Sometimes, you catch the current just right, and it's a surprise.

You wrote because you wanted to write, and people found your work. More people than ever before. It feels like an avalanche, but eventually, you hit the shore, and you don't quite know where you've been or how far you've traveled. This experience can feel discombobulating, and in our experience, you do well to let your body and mind play catch up. Celebrate what felt good, and write down what you learned.

Know that it might have been a once-in-a-lifetime experience, but it could just as easily happen again next week.

Our (brief) A-Z of Substack

A. Add your Substack to Google Console, which means it's more likely to show up in the search engine. Think about your 'about' page and the fact that if someone is reading in the app, it's the ONE place to link to your most brilliant articles and other things.
B. Be brave and publish your first post—send a friend a preview first if you'd like. Then, boost—our advice—make sure this is turned on in your settings! Substack will automatically apply a 20% discount to paid memberships for your most engaged subs...
C. Comment on other people's work—spend time replying to your comments too. Factor those slots in; they are super important. A co-created experience pushes our limits and takes us out of the echo chamber. It's also the secret sauce of taking us out of our own heads into the real world of where our work is landing!
D. Devote some time to filling in the bits and pieces in your settings! Try 20-minute slots a few times over a month, and you'll soon have it all done.
E. Evolve as a writer, as a creator, as a co-creator, as a person. Substack and the world it's created have a lot to teach us about humanity, privilege, and taking up space in the world in a place that allows us space and doesn't choke our words with an algorithm.
F. Find your flow. It can take a little while, but stay creative with that process...don't give up. Work at your pace, but don't abandon yourself—what you have to share and say is important!
G. Go Paid! You can set monthly, annual, and founding member prices. Remember, Substack takes 10%
H. Headers and Footers—if your people are reading in the app, they won't see these, so I use them as an invite to join Substack. I'd also say stay honest about how it's all feeling, what you're struggling with, what you are questioning. Not only is that a clear path to your intuition, but there'll also be someone to help if you shout about it.
I. Import your emails, your old blogs, etc. Bring your old content and

your existing subs here to start the Substack snowball effect. Tell your subscribers what you are doing and why, and the rest will work itself out.

J. Join some supportive communities. There are hundreds, if not thousands. Take your pick. Want to chat with people about baking, gardens, politics, and the stock exchange? Go wild!
K. Keep going—settle into a cadence that works for you! This took me months and months, but I get it now. One less decision to make = more time to write!
L. Leave space for reading other Substacks. Be of service to your community.
M. Make space to learn, but be discerning who you learn from.
N. Notifications—turn off unsubscribes—thank me for that one later! Keep it manageable. We are not meant to be responding to notifications left, right, and center—it upsets our nervous systems and our dopamine levels.
O. Open your emails! If you need to subscribe to less, turn on 'smart notifications' and read in the Substack app instead.
P. Pick up guests and collaborations. Collaborations are a BRILLIANT way to grow your Substack audience. They also offer scope to explore how you work with another writer/creative. There are lots of approaches to collaborations. Here are a few we love: guest post hop, multiple guests post hop, multiple guests post invitation, and cross-post. You can also host your podcast on Substack for free and pull the RSS feed through to other spaces like Apple Music and Spotify.
Q. Question your reason for creating/writing here—what's your why, and what's your long-term why? My favorite set of questions to ask myself and stay clear on is: is creating in congruence like setting your creativity on fire? Do this exercise and report back, or join our paid communities. We go deep into this stuff and support each other.
R. Recommend the Substacks you LOVE to read! Spend a little time each month writing blurbs for other writers. You can use the 'referral' button to ask folks to refer folks to your Substack and set

the terms of your digital gifts.

S. Stats—you'll get a monthly stats email, but also head here to check what is working for you in promoting your publication and where in the world folks are reading it. & Sections—make sure you tick 'add all your existing subs' if you start a new section; they can take themselves out later.

T. True—be true to yourself. Grow into this space, take up space, "create the thing you wish existed", and take your community with you. There are no rules, so don't seek them out; own your voice, create!

U. Understand that growth takes time. Virality is a thing that happens to people—you don't have to strive for that. If you do accidentally have it happen, it will bring a ton of noise with it... Trust the noise will die down, and everything will be calm again.

V. Very sparkly. Sparkle up your Substack experience! And remember, Substack has a Help article for absolutely EVERYTHING! Just google it or use the search function on either of our publications.

W. Write, just write and make it feel good. Get rid of everything that gets in the way of your writer. Make friends with your Writer Dashboard! Spend some time with your welcome page.

X. eXclude anything that doesn't make you feel good—we don't need a popularity contest to collect publications here—make sure you curate this space as you would a beautiful garden party for your favorite person's birthday!

Y. Ask questions—can I get away with that for "Y" in a book about writers' platforms? Check what your subscribers are reading and who your top commenters are. Get to know what's resonating—it's all in the back office for you to see.

Z. Zzzzz—someone is awake somewhere in the world and on Substack reading your brilliant work—and we're done!

Let's create a timeline we are proud of...

A note from Russell

When I started working with Claire, even though she had 1,500+ subscribers and I had 20,000+, we were on similar paid subscriber journeys. She has far fewer subscribers than I do, but the engagement she gets in her community is bonkers. While I have a respectable 2% engagement on my most popular posts, she regularly pulls 20% in her community. Her articles are filled with 200+ comment articles, and it boggles my mind.

I hired Claire to help boost engagement in my community and tested a lot of her concepts in early 2024. Her ideas make me very uncomfortable, but she is an engagement genius. I enthusiastically support her Sparkle Audit, which will pull you out of your comfort zone in the best ways possible. She also provides a free 5-day course you can get.

I love her Sparkle on Substack publication. The rest of this chapter is about her story.

Claire's story

Let me tell you a story about building an audience from scratch.

Everyone knows someone who knows someone, right? But what if you want to start from zero? Or build your writing and creative craft as you grow with new people seeing your work?

What if you also want to reach inboxes all over the globe? All times of the day and night?

With Substack, you can, and I did! For the very first time in my 20-year career.

I began my journey with Substack in April 2022. I wrote a little, dug around, and read some pieces from some great (and intimidatingly brilliant) writers.

I got to know the platform, the team who made it, and the ethics behind it. It quickly started to feel like home.

In December of the same year, I removed all other 'social apps' from my phone, showed up at Substack Writers Open Office Hours and read every single comment.

I was fascinated by how people saw the platform, its plus points and limitations, and the questions they had. I chatted a little with people there; they were warm and friendly. I was surprised. Lots of them subscribed to my publication. I saw the spikes on my subscriber graph the next day.

Later that same year, I brought my mailing list of 300 over from MailChimp and then grew my spaces to 3,000 by the following summer (2023).

Here's the breakdown of that period, as much as I can remember. I'm an open book here about Substack.

- **April '22**—I was influenced by my husband, David Venus, who is an 'early adopter' of tech. I started a Substack, wrote on Substack, and turned on the option for folks to pay to read my paywalled content. People paid. I decided I better write something behind a paywall.

- **April to September '22**—I got curious about what Substack is and read a lot of US Substacks from writers I'd never heard of and some UK ones, including Emma Gannon at The Hyphen and Things Worth Knowing with Farrah Storr. People kept referencing Heather Cox Richardson; I noted she was the creator of the highest-selling Substack.

- **Summer '22**—I started to see 'writer/influencer names' coming over to the platform. Perhaps Substack was supporting them or they had a gang together? They were instantly good at using the platform. I could learn from them. They kept coming, and I kept learning.

- **September '22**—I imported my mailing list (x300 people). I explained I would now send their monthly email from Substack and other posts, too.

- **November '22**—I started to see checkmarks next to writers' names.

- **September '22 to February '23**—I wrote consistently and started to make some contacts and friends here on Substack. I switched up my Instagram to talk about my Substack (3500 followers).

- **February '23**—First viral post: 'Is Substack a Side Hustle?'

- **March '23**—I taught a webinar/masterclass: 'Get Creative on Substack' online on zoom.

- **April '23**—I launched a second Substack, a 'slow grow' community for mothers, and a podcast with Laura Oldfield over at Company of Two.

- **May '23**—I started a YouTube playlist called Joyful Growth on Substack to teach some of what I was learning and see how it landed with an adjacent audience. I searched what others were teaching and noted it was VERY different from my style.

- **April to July '23**—I wrote a (pretty much) weekly 'Get Creative on Substack' post to help my artist pals I'd brought over and to stop all the WhatsApp and email questions. I experimented with audio. I noted I had less than 1000 subscribers but more than 600 listens to my audio pieces.

- **July '23**—I launched a new publication, Sparkle on Substack, and a paid members community for folks who wanted to 'Stay Creative on Substack' and get Substack education from me. Embedded a podcast as part of the space. Hit 2000 subscribers.

- **October '23**—I got a Substack bestseller badge (101 paid subs).

- **November '23**—Podcasted with Russell Nohelty, hit $10k gross annualized revenue on Sparkle. Added that to the revenue on Creatively Conscious and realized it was $12.5k gross annualized revenue.

- **December '23**—Celebrated steady growth of 500 subs a month across both publications (Sparkle x 400, Creatively Conscious x 100) for four months in a row. Almost at 4500 subscribers and 190 paid overall.

This isn't a chapter about my highlights reel, although it is meant to inspire, of course.

I want to talk to you about depth of connection, inspiration, storytelling, and meaningful engagement.

Why? Because that's where the growth actually is. That's what was really going on behind the scenes of the timeline above. I was writing AND building community. That's the USP of both of my publications, and that's my 'unfair advantage'.

Generosity breeds growth. It's that simple. I could mention more tips, and I will, but if you remember this one, you'll fly. I guarantee it.

So, are you ready to be generous with your words, your reading time, and your interactions? Who's publication might you start with? How about right here?

When I imported my subs from MailChimp, I had reason to show up, reason to write, and reason to be of service. As far as I know, none of the people from MailChimp were using Substack, but I didn't need them to be. I just needed a place for my words to land, a place to tell my stories. We all need that, but we all started from one. Write for one person, and you'll soon write for hundreds.

I read the names of my subscribers often, some of whom I knew in real life. None of them were my commissioners. Lots of them were my colleagues, some were my husband's clients, some knew me through artist residencies, and some I'd met on Instagram.

Subscriptions but not as we know them?

In March 2023, I ran a masterclass called "Get Creative on Substack". I charged £15 for it, and over 50 people bought it. I was genuinely so excited about Substack and my sector using it. Guess what happened, and here's the important part...

After the class, the majority of the participants came right over to Substack and started playing around.

They already knew how to use the platform and supported my work and my Substack instantly. Remember, I was already generous with my likes and comments...and so I taught them to do that, too. It's not a hack. It's a belief system...

They asked for more tips on writing, generosity, creativity, and authenticity. I gave them what they wanted in more posts about Substack and how I was using it. In those posts, I shared the creativity of how others were using it, too.

My subscribers on Substack, especially those who pay, are not passive followers of my work. They are, for the most part, cheerleaders of it, and I am of theirs (where I can be).

De-mystifying Substack is part of our job if we want success here. It's not unique to me; we all have to do it because it's a complex platform and people think they know 'social media' and newsletters. They might, but they don't know Substack. It's different here.

You want your subscribers to reply to your Substack Notes, get involved in your Substack Chats, write comments on your posts, and listen to and share your audio. That's the goal.

I know my subscribers well; they hunt out my email, write to me and ask for more advice or to work with me 1-2-1. They are on my LinkedIn group; they aren't afraid to ask questions.

Most of my paid subscribers are (nearly) my friends

I've met a handful of them in real life. It's worth noting that your "online persona" has an energy all of its own, which lacks nuance because it's a hologram in your readers' hive mind. The bits they build up of you matter.

I've cultivated a community that wants to ride the snowy slopes of Substack Mountain alongside me. They'll use their binoculars to see what's on the horizon, and they are NOT waiting for someone to give them a free ride or for them to go viral!

They are here to explore, discover and rediscover their craft. To get creative here, to be in the community. I can be an expert with them, but I can also be an ally.

Curiosity is key to growth. Leaning into it, fascinating in it, and getting to know yourself and your readers better. There are so many ways to do that here.

One of the best ways I've found is to share a little piece of your heart with every single post! To tell your story, your real story (in part) every single time you write...

Pausing for Northumberland storytime...

I love real, relatable stories, so I need to pause to reference the congruence in all of this; otherwise, it's just an un-relatable growth post where you say, "Yes, Claire, that's all very well and good for you, but what about me?"

So here's what really happened. As well as everything else I've talked about. Here's the real stuff, the visceral, tangible world of my life.

In 2020, my whole world turned upside down when my husband got gravely sick in the last weeks of my pregnancy with my second child. The doctors didn't know what was wrong, and we were on the long list for a hospital referral in a pandemic while he couldn't leave our bed. The week I was due to give birth, we got Covid. Then his turned into Long Covid, and there was more darkness than we had ever known.

At that time, I showed up online in the messy and complex world I was in.

On the glossy perfectionist-driven world of Instagram, people turned away when I showed up wild-eyed and talked about the pressure of having a newborn and a sick husband. On Substack, people leaned in, asked questions, and held me in it.

I wrote about some of it on Substack. The people who knew me online at Creatively Conscious were even more supportive of my launching an online teaching space at Sparkle on Substack 14 months later. They were in awe of me, proud of me and—here's the important part—genuinely happy for the success it brought. They were like that because I was honest and transparent in my writing.

This matters.

It matters because it was a time of tension on Substack, and it will be again.

Jealousy often comes from not understanding the whole human in a success story. If we are jealous, we withhold our support. I had the opposite. I had an outpouring of support and some of it fiercely so.

There are multiple educators now, but at that time, there were just a few and many opinions about that. It was BOLD to say I'm starting a second Substack, and it was even bolder to set out that it was a dedicated teaching space from an unpublished writer (me) on a platform set up for writers.

I was still showing up unmasked and complicated over at Creatively Conscious, and I honestly believe the reason I'm supported and celebrated here at all is because one person started.

One person understood enough to see what a bold move it was, and they told some friends, and they invited their friends, who then invited their colleagues, and that's why I am growing the way I am.

The people who 'knew me' chose to support me and my work not once but every single time they saw it.

The time is now, my friends. Are you coming with us? There's space for you, I promise. Before you do...

If all the world is (really) a stage...

Shakespeare wrote 'As You Like It' in 1599.

That's 423 years ago—over four centuries of human evolution and possibility and learning about creativity. The internet came to be in my last year of school. I mostly ignored it, and now I spend my working days on it. I'd recommend Shakespeare to anyone...would you?

Substack has invited us to take up space in a way other platforms have never managed it. More than that, the culture of the platform keeps making the same invite day in and day out until we take it, until we put our words to the page, until we make our heart-fuelled creations real.

Anyone can start a Substack. It's a storytelling tool, not a marketing tool; that's its main job. That's what some people miss when they start here.

I don't know if Shakespeare worried about what people thought of his art, of his words, of his way of seeing the world before he released them. Perhaps the words flowed through him, and he, like some of us, knew he was guided to write them by a force bigger than himself.

Let Substack set your stage. There's really not much difference between Shakespeare and Substack; they were just born at different times.

They are both vehicles for creativity, admiration, enjoyment, fandom, and community. They both set the stage for us and are open to interpretation.

I often wonder if Substack built their model of generosity with great artists and word crafters in mind... I'd recommend Substack to anyone. Would you?

The thing you have to do here is to know that your readers are coming and that your supporters are ready. It just takes a little time. Shakespeare wasn't an overnight success, and you don't have to be either, but you do have to use the recommendations tool here on Substack.

Waiting for the invite...the duality of being a human online.

On Substack, I've felt as wise as an elder and like a toddler in a tantrum.

I've been both the cool kid and the one who sat alone at parties.

In my career, I've got the dream job and never even gotten a callback. I've turned heads in the street and been cheated on by multiple ex-lovers.

All the worlds of a shapeshifter are also true on Substack because, and here's the kicker, humans are intrinsically complex, and Substack is the first platform to make space for that and cheerlead it at the very same time.

You can show up as your authentic self here, and if you choose not to, people see that lack of congruence a mile away.

Let me explain, and we can get practical at the same time...

Notes, but give it some depth...

When Substack Notes launched, we all saw our publications grow if we used it. I rode that wave, and I still show up there every single day. People will have pressed the mute button, and that's fine.

At the end of March '23, my publication sat at 541 subscribers. At the end of May '23, it had 878 subscribers. That's 337 extra subs. I'll take the unsubscribes and the mutes in the mix.

This is all from using Notes. It took me six years to grow 300 email subscribers on Substack. I used Notes for six weeks and 300 beautiful souls connected with me and gave me their email.

It's worth saying that during the week Notes launched, I got a note featured by Substack Reads.

The focus is on conversation and building community.

There are 3 strands to my intention with Substack Notes:

1. Creative community building

2. Visibility (for my publications) and

3. Play.

They are unique to me and the way I create, but you can borrow them if you like.

You do not have to be good

Making space for rejection and the tumbleweed of a post with no 'likes' or 'comments' is hard. But if you cultivate support here first, the support for your work comes naturally.

You can't sit and wait for the invite here, you've got to get out there and cheerlead and support others. You have to build community and find common threads with others. Collaborate, chat, reply. People have to know who you are and what you're about.

The first time I had a post 'do well', it was about Substack (the previously mentioned Side Hustle post).

It brought more likes and comments than I'd ever known. It was like a rapturous applause - I felt it in my cells; it felt nice.

My biggest lesson this year is that I don't have to be liked by everyone. I come back to the words of Mary Oliver in her poem Wild Geese, and I keep showing up multiple times a week for the people who find my words, my classes, and my tutorials an act of service.

It's enough.

Our sacred creativity is a portal into our wisest selves. People want that. They are here for it. They crave connection to the tribe we've lost online or otherwise.

I know because I am them.

My 5 top tips for increasing engagement for your Substack publication

- Read other Substacks you are genuinely interested in—be generous and let people know you're there. Feel compelled to like or reply to someone else's comment? Do it! Don't hesitate! Start a conversation, keep going, and dedicate time to this. Be authentic, not like an awkward robot.

- Be abundant in your support in sharing what's working for you here, generous in your intention, and gently curious in your challenges. Don't boss anyone around. We are all experimenting and learning from each other all the time.

- Read the room, then write on Substack Notes with your writer name. Don't use "Kitty365" or a complex publication name—no one will remember you. Use your name and feel the replies. Start conversations there. Chime in with others, and have fun! Notes is a 24/7 conversation, not a bulletin board; use it that way.

- Use polls in posts and look at the results; reflect the results back to a handful of your readers privately and ask again. Get into conversations with your top readers... You can find this information in your *subscribers* tab. Every single article they have opened and read is there for you to geek out over.

- Cross-pollinate and know you won't be for everyone, and people might actively turn against your work. You might trigger them—it's all ok. It's not your job to convince people to love you or your work. That's coming anyway! Use the recommendations tool wholeheartedly and be generous in your blurbs there.

Recommendations

Words mean something.

There are multiple stories about the origin of an engagement ring, but I like the one about why we wear it on our left finger.

It was thought this finger had a direct line to the heart. In being engaged and wearing a ring as a symbol of that, we were more connected to our heart space, to love.

Ask yourself—could you bring more of your heart through your hands as you type your work, write your replies, support others...

As you are sharing your words, you get to think about where they will land. Will they be in congruence?

Of course, not everyone will come to your word in an embodied and calm state, BUT ask yourself how you want them to feel opening up your Substack.

Intrigued?

Held? Curious? Creative? Soothed? Educated?

Part of something special?

How can you be a diamond in someone's day? That's what we strive for.

I ask myself, will this piece, this work, this part of my heart send a prism of rainbow light through my reader's day?

Will it make their heart dance with creative possibility? Will it blow their mind? Will it blind them temporarily in a breathless pause? Will they feel connected, cherished, and safe with me? Will they feel compelled to reply here or in another online portal? Will they feel less alone?

Will we be friends?

No one wants to be alone. Being alone is as close to the edge as we can be.

Online is real, and loneliness is tangible online. That's why people stop. That's why they stop sharing their heart, their words, their creations.

That's why people complain about likes (or lack thereof) and compare themselves to others. If you don't want to be or feel alone, you have to help others to feel less alone first. You have to engage. Lead with curiosity and reciprocity.

How Substack fits into the future of traditional and other forms of publishing

We believe the future of publishing is selling directly to readers, technology-assisted, community-driven, distributing your work widely across many platforms, immersive, and decentralized. Let's see how Substack fits into that narrative.

Does Substack help you sell direct to readers?

The short answer to this question is yes, but it's worth spending a second talking about what direct-to-readers means inside the publishing landscape. Direct sales work on a spectrum between a platform like Patreon that lets you interact with your readers and collect their email addresses but handles the payment processing themselves, all the way to setting up a booth at a trade show where you collect the money directly from the person buying from you and get to shake their hand.

For me, there are three areas by which I think about selling directly to readers.

- Does this platform allow me to interact directly with readers without a middleman?

- Does this platform allow me to collect customer data and offer interoperability so I can take them to another platform without much hassle if I ever choose or am forced to leave?

- Does this platform allow me to process payments through my own processors, like Stripe, Thrivecart, or Square, or do they process payments themselves?

Does Substack allow me to interact directly with readers without a middleman?

When I first started thinking about direct sales, I only used the second and third questions to define direct sales. However, when I talked to writers over the last several months, they often incorrectly conflated platforms like Facebook or Reddit with direct sales.

I've heard many cases of why Facebook is a great direct sales marketplace, but after my Facebook account was locked and access to my 15,000+ Facebook fans and 1,800 friends was revoked in an instant, I became living proof that you only have direct access to your readers on most platforms until they decide to rip them away from you. Social media platforms will always act as an intermediary between you and your fans.

Yes, I had access directly to them through comments and messages, but only through the app and website. I couldn't access their buyer data or even their customer data. I didn't even have access to their emails unless they chose to share them. In every case, they act as a middleman.

Facebook acts as an intermediary in the distribution chain between the customer and me. Since they don't give me access to my customer's data or offer interoperability between myself and my subscribers, or even my friends, I have decided that social media networks, by and large, are not good channels for direct sales.

Substack, on the other hand, doesn't have that restraint. While I don't have access to somebody's email until they subscribe, once they do, I have customer data associated with their account. The ability to follow an account with subscribing muddies this, and I might change my opinion in the future, but right now, I believe Substack Notes is a great avenue for cultivating direct sales.

Does Substack allow me to collect customer data and offer interoperability so I can take them to another platform without much hassle?

The next question I ask is not only whether I can collect customer or subscriber data on the platform but whether it allows me to download that data quickly if I choose to move off the platform.

In this scenario, Substack also shines. I download my entire email list from Substack every month, and it's as simple as going to DASHBOARD>SUBSCRIBERS>EXPORT.

While it takes a few minutes to come through since I have quite a few subscribers at this point, I can get them with near immediacy.

Does Substack allow me to process payments through my own processors, like Stripe, Thrivecart, or Square, or do they process payments themselves?

The one advantage of having a platform like Patreon handle payments for you is that they handle the sales tax for your publication as well. Using your preferred payment processor makes you liable for sales tax in states where you have a sales nexus.

This is even more complicated by the fact that every state, and country for that matter, defines a sales nexus differently. Luckily, because Substack integrates with Stripe, there is a solution for this headache. Stripe has a service called StripeTax that will do much of this for you.

I vastly prefer working with a platform that allows me to collect payments through my preferred processor because when you want to change platforms, it is very easy to connect those buyers with another service. Assuming any new platform also integrates with Stripe, I can connect my buyers and their existing payment information to my new platform with little effort.

When you use a platform like Patreon, it's very hard to move off the platform without completely breaking your payment system and losing paying members in the process. I have friends who have a Patreon and another service, like Ream, because they simply can't cut off their payments on Patreon without destroying their entire business.

In this way, Substack shines for a third time. They are not a perfect direct sales platform, especially since they don't offer the ability to sell other products or have a storefront. However, as a direct sales platform, Substack is very well-positioned to become a major player in the future of publishing.

That said, Substack is probably not able to be your only direct sales platform. While they are great for building a paid newsletter, that is only one part of direct sales. When Monica and I talk about direct sales we speak across several different aspects.

- Crowdfunding
- Memberships ←**This is where Substack fits in.**
- Web store
- Special offers
- Sales Funnels
- Conventions

While Substack is great for a paid newsletter, the fact they only allow for one or two tiers limits them in ways even a simple platform like Kofi doesn't. Their laser focus on one type of customer has given them incredible clarity of vision, but it's unlikely you'll be able to grow a sustainable business without integrating other platforms and services into your business.

That's not necessarily a bad thing. I've been a huge advocate for Kickstarter for almost a decade, and they don't integrate easily with any other major direct sales platform, either. Still, I've raised close to $500,000 on Kickstarter, and we've helped authors raise $1.2 million through crowdfunding since launching the Kickstarter Accelerator in January 2022.

(One side note about Kickstarter. Even though their system integrates with Stripe, they collect all the pledges for you inside their account and send them in one bulk payment. Just one of the little quirks of direct sales proving every system works a bit differently.)

Being hyperfocused is how businesses scale, but as you think about growing your publication, Substack will likely need to be augmented with something else or many other things.

For instance, I launch several Kickstarters a year, have a web store, a Teachable site, table at conventions, run special offers to my newsletters, teach courses, and write this Substack, among other things. Meanwhile, on top of Stripe, I also have payment processing through Thrivecart, Square, and Paypal, along with Venmo and the Cash app.

All that together gives me a stable income, but more proof that no one solution is a magic bullet.

Does Substack embrace technology to help its users thrive?

Putting aside for a minute the fact that Substack allows you the option to generate AI imagery *(even though it's slow and cumbersome),* what I'm trying to get at with this question is whether a platform takes advantage of technological advancements in a way that helps their users build more sustainable businesses.

Yes, it could include AI imagery if that improves your flow, but what I'm really after is whether you can rely on the platform to integrate with new technologies in a smart, intuitive way. Lots of platforms will add new technology without forethought, which makes the overall user experience significantly worse for writers.

Substack, by contrast, seems to spend an inordinate amount of time thinking about what users really need before they integrate something into their service. For instance, while I don't agree with their stance on offering an advertising platform like Beehiiv or Sparkloop, I do appreciate that they have thought extensively about these solutions and have an ethos about why they haven't gone that way...yet.

It helps me trust that the things they do integrate will be worthwhile. This year saw the introduction of Notes, which has helped me grow exponentially in just the last couple of months since it launched. It's also vastly improved the on-site experience for me in the long run because it helps me find new creators to read and add them to my network.

They also introduced an entirely new dashboard in May, which has helped me understand my audiences better. You might think that these things don't count as technology because they don't use the words AI in them, but since different types of AI power every platform and algorithm, I would disagree with you on that. Notes, even though it is basic, still uses an algorithm to determine what you see and what you don't.

I've worked with companies that don't take a measured approach with their integrations, and my confidence quickly eroded in them until the relationship deteriorated. They moved quickly, broke things, and destroyed my experience on the platform. It's nice to be on a platform that, while I don't always agree with them, has a consistent stance on technological integrations into their user experience.

I should mention that while I tend to agree with Substack on how they integrate technology into their platform, that agreement does not extend to their moderation policy or the types of people they sometimes promote on their platform.

Does Substack facilitate community on their platform?

Just like with direct sales, there are a couple of metrics I use to judge community on a platform.

- Does the platform allow interaction between readers and writers?

- Does the platform help discoverability across their platform for new users to find publications?

- Does the platform allow users to interact with the corporate entity to give feedback to improve the experience?

- Does the platform allow creators to form strong bonds to work together on common projects for their users?

- Does the platform protect its users through best practices on content moderation?

Does Substack allow interaction between readers and writers?

Between comments on articles, chats, and notes, Substack allows no less than three different ways to facilitate interaction between writers and their readers, allowing for even more interaction through restacking, mentions, and crossposting. While none of these are spectacularly novel innovations, Substack makes it as easy as any platform I've ever seen to foster interaction between readers and writers. It also allows writers control of whether to open comments to all readers or paid subscribers and the ability to block trolls from your publication. I wish that they had a more active moderation policy, though.

Does Substack help discoverability across their platform for new users to find publications?

With their Search tab, Notes functionality, and Substack Reads newsletter, Substack has a top-down approach to helping writers find more readers for their publication. While they have a lot of avenues for discoverability, they seem mostly focused on promoting successful publications and influencers, which makes sense because those are the ones that make money for them.

Still, they do give smaller publications some tools to help discoverability as well. These outlets offer ways for publications of any size to find new publications and create networking opportunities. Additionally, authors can band together to create a group project or a group publication like Fictionistas.

Does Substack allow users to interact with the corporate entity to give feedback to improve the experience?

Yes. Inside every publication is a chat widget you can use to connect to Substack support. It's like a WhatsApp chat, and you can choose the filter for free, paid, or founding members.

Does Substack allow creators to form strong bonds to work together on common projects for their users?

While customer support is a failing of Substack, where they shine is facilitating strong bonds between writers. On top of simply fostering interaction between publications, you can very easily add guest writers to your publication or even create a new publication with multiple authors. I would love to be able to combine multiple disparate publications into one subscription, like Bundlerabbit allows with anthologies, and have the money distributed to each other in the backend, but Substack is a relatively small team, and I know they only have so much bandwidth.

Does the platform protect its users through best practices on content moderation?

I can't in good conscience conclude this section without mentioning that Substack's moderation policies are onerous to publications, and the people they choose to promote sometimes show a complete lack of compassion for under-recognized groups. I have watched marginalized writers get harassed incessantly on Substack for posting well-researched articles. I have watched the same trolls pop up again and again on different writer publications, even though they should have been banned long ago. The brunt of the moderation burden should be borne by the platform, not the users.

Even though I didn't agree with their policy in the pre-Notes days, maintaining it after launching a social media network to encourage interaction between users shows a lack of care for marginalized voices, and the tone-deaf public attitude from the corporate brass forces me to couch my glowing approval of the platform and the people who run it with a thick layer of trepidation.

There are a lot of incredible voices on Substack, and in the pockets I live in, I rarely see any of this bubble up, but then again, I am a het, cis, white male who was rarely called to task by trolls, even on other platforms. I have talked to publications that deal with harassment all the time and have personally watched it happen enough that it sours my otherwise great experience with the platform. I'm not talking about negative comments, either. I'm talking about truly vile things and threats that any platform should rush to ban.

Does Substack help writers distribute their work more widely?

In 2014, Amazon introduced Kindle Unlimited, allowing authors to make money when somebody "borrowed" their book from their library while requiring exclusivity to Amazon for ebooks.

After this, the conversation became about whether you were going into KU (Kindle Unlimited) or going wide with your work.

Why do so many authors enroll in KDP Select?

Authors enroll in KDP Select because it allows them to make money without the reader purchasing their book. Since the subscriber pays a single monthly fee, anything they read, which is available in the program, is absolutely free...and getting somebody to try a free thing is way easier than getting somebody to pay for something.

Since the entry cost for a Kindle Unlimited book is nothing for the subscriber, and since Kindle Unlimited readers are generally voracious readers, the odds that they will try any book offered to them in their genre are very high. As a quick note, longer books tend to do better in KDP Select because people have to read many more pages to complete them. If you write short novels, the benefits of KDP select will be reduced considerably, but they may still make sense for you.

What does "going wide" with a book launch mean?

The other option for authors when planning their book launch is to "go wide". What does going wide mean? It means that instead of enrolling in KDP Select, an author chooses to place their book on all platforms, including but not limited to iBooks, Amazon, Nook, and Kobo, among many others. There are dozens, maybe hundreds, of places an author can choose to distribute their books.

Uploading your book to so many places might sound daunting, but there are services like Smashwords and Draft2Digital that can upload your books to most major platforms for you, so you only have to upload your book once. However, there are caveats to this, which we will discuss below.

Notice that when you "go wide", you will also be uploading your book to Amazon. You will just not be enrolling it into the KDP Select program. It is a common misnomer that going wide precludes you from publishing your book on Amazon, but that is not the case. It means you are publishing on other platforms in addition to Amazon.

Why would anybody go wide with their book launch?

If Kindle Unlimited is so amazing and can pay you for letting people read your book for free, why would anybody do anything else? Well, the reasons are varied, but the main one deals with exclusivity. When you enroll in Kindle Unlimited, you agree that your book will not be available for purchase ANYWHERE else, including your own website. Enrollment periods last for 90 days, which means you are tied to the Amazon platform exclusively for three months.

That means your book will only be available on Amazon and only available on Kindle Unlimited in the USA, UK, Germany, France, Italy, Spain, India, China, Japan, Brazil, Mexico, Canada, and Australia.

Since Amazon is over 80% of the ebook market, that doesn't sound so bad, right?

Maybe, except that Amazon is only 80% of the USA-based market. In many other countries, it is not the most popular, and in some countries, it's not even second place. This is a problem if you want to have a global footprint with your books since people in many other countries often don't even register Amazon as a viable option.

Additionally, some readers simply hate Amazon and won't deal with them, even in the USA, so you are alienating yourself from those readers by not giving them the option to purchase your books.

From 2014-2022, the industry overwhelmingly told authors to release their books in KU because they made more money, even if they had to lock their books away in the Amazon vault and play by their rules.

While 90%+ of authors still launch their books in KU, the industry is changing. Last year, I was at a conference where nearly every author was considering going wide, which was the first time I had seen that in all my years working with writers.

This is different for other types of writers, of course, and many don't even release books or don't release them independently. Blog authors usually syndicate their work to multiple platforms to increase reach, and comics never had a gatekeeper like Amazon that forced exclusivity, which allowed them to cross-post from the beginning.

(I should mention that while you can syndicate a blog, almost all platforms at this point prefer native uploads over syndication as this is shown in their backend as unique content—even when it isn't—and thus increases the platform's value to users and investors.)

What excites me about Substack is the burgeoning fiction community that serializes their work on Substack. Between The Library, Talebones, Erica Drayton, Fictionistas, and dozens of other authors, along with comic book writers like Scott Snyder, Substack is helping create a new path for writers to monetize their work.

The serial fiction community has Royal Road, Wattpad, and Radish, among others, but with each of them, you are relying on their platform and their ever-changing compensation metrics to grow. Meanwhile, Medium is geared more toward nonfiction, while Webtoon and Tapas for comics also don't allow for direct sales. There are vanishingly few ways for somebody to serialize their work and grow their own direct sales audience with fiction outside of Substack.

Additionally, Substack has an RSS reader that allows your readers to pull other blogs into one world-class reading format, helping increase the ever-important time-on-site metric.

We believe the future of publishing is not just publishing wide on platforms outside of Amazon but going wider than wide with platforms like Substack, Kickstarter, and others that allow you to control your buyer data and get paid for your work directly.

Even though I do believe that Substack is great for fiction authors who are wide with their work, this is not necessarily the same for nonfiction authors because you can't easily syndicate a Substack article. With your blog, you can syndicate your work to other platforms like Medium, but if you write an article for Substack, you have to do the work to republish it and reformat it for syndication on another platform, which is a pain.

Part of that is because Substack does not have an open API, so nothing can connect to it. I get why they made that choice. APIs are expensive time-sucks, by and large, but I would be remiss if I didn't mention that it was a concern.

Does Substack help provide an immersive experience to readers?

What does the word immersive even mean when it comes to the future of publishing? Virtual reality and, to a lesser extent, augmented reality are both clearly immersive, but so is a brand like Star Wars that covers a hundred different formats and even has its own theme park experience.

When I think of immersive in the context of a platform like Substack, what I look for is whether it encourages readers to happily spend hours on the platform and whether it allows writers to provide unique experiences to readers they can't get anywhere else.

With Substack, I think of Geoffrey Golden and his Substack Adventure Snack, where he provides readers with short, choose-your-own-adventure experiences every week. I think of the potential for writers to augment their universe with additional short stories. I think of people offering paid bonus content to their members and ways that allow readers to fall even further down the rabbit hole of a publication they love. I think of the ability to provide coaching calls so people can meet with authors in person, as well as other unique experiences that people have only begun scratching the surface of up until now.

While most writers aren't utilizing the immersive qualities of Substack, and even I have a hard time conceiving what they will be, the potential is there. I hope the platform continues to build out the possibility for immersive content in the future.

Does Substack provide a decentralized experience to users?

The short answer to this is yes...kinda. Before I go further, I should mention that, in this case, I'm not talking about blockchain specifically. I'm talking about the ability of a writer to build and control an experience for their readers outside of centralized control—the more control a writer has of the reader experience, the more decentralized the platform.

While this can happen with blockchain, the concept of decentralization has existed since the dawn of business. Barnes and Noble decentralized a lot of their decision-making to local stores, for instance.

Decentralization is referred to as a form of an organizational structure where there is a delegation of authority by the top management to the middle and lower levels of management in an organization.

In this type of organizational structure, the duty of daily operations and minor decision-making capabilities are transferred to the middle and lower levels, which allows top-level management to focus more on major decisions like business expansion, diversification etc.

Delegation refers to the assignment of a portion of work and the associated responsibility by a superior to a subordinate. In simple words, when delegation is expanded on an organizational level, it is called decentralization.

Like almost everything else we have talked about so far, decentralization lives on a vast spectrum. Barnes and Noble gives store managers some control, but they still have to answer to a centralized corporate entity. Owning a franchise like McDonald's gives you more control than working at Barnes and Noble, and becoming an approved partner to sell something like Verizon phones in your own store gives you even more control than either of those. Meanwhile, joining your local chamber of commerce gives you even greater control of your own business while still allowing you to access some resources of a centralized collective.

The same is true online. While Substack does allow writers to create their own publications and even use their own domain to cater to a unique experience, this is still nowhere near the boundary of where decentralization can take you.

I tend to agree with Simon Owens that Substack's unfair advantage is how it combines the decentralization of having siloed newsletters that don't talk to each other with a recommendation engine and social media experience that brings people together in one place. He also pinpoints the problem with true decentralization.

The advantage of something like Notes is that you can easily go from the centralized social media platform to a more decentralized newsletter at the push of a single subscribe button. Substack has taken the best parts of decentralization (owning the customer data) and combined it with the best parts of social media (a hub by which to share ideas).

This is especially interesting because while many platforms tout true decentralization, the experience of being siloed away from everyone else kind of sucks. However, centralization is also problematic because then you are at the whim of the algorithm. I don't know if Substack strikes the right balance, but it's close.

If you can't tell by the tenor of this post, I'm bullish on Substack now and in the future as an important cog in the publishing landscape. While it's not perfect, I think the positives vastly outweigh the negatives, even though the negatives are certainly worth considering before you go all in on the platform.

It's probably worth setting up a publication for the organic newsletter growth alone. In the past 30 days, I've had 622 new subscribers to my publication without spending a dime. With paid newsletter growth strategies, you could be paying anywhere from $1-$10 to acquire a new email, so that is a ton of real-world value Substack provides for writers.

At the end of the day, what can Substack tell us about the future of publishing? I think it can show other platforms how to create an environment for writers to thrive. The next 3-5 years will be about taking control of your customer data and owning the experience you provide to your fans.

This might be scary to some people, but it also means that you can stop paying middlemen and keep more of the money you rightly earned from your work. The best platforms will combine the ability to own the customer data with an algorithm that encourages discoverability. Even when I don't post a new article, I gain at least 5-10 new subscribers a day on my Substack, and that is growth that used to either go to a platform or I had to pay dearly for through advertising.

This is the kind of experience I hope to find throughout the future of publishing, as people lose patience with centralized platforms but don't have the infrastructure to build their own web store experiences. Kickstarter strikes a great balance between empowering discoverability across its platform and keeping each project siloed in its own bubble. I think Substack might do a better job than Kickstarter. As a devoted Kickstarter fanboy, even considering such a thing is a big deal, let alone writing it down.

It's still a nascent platform for fiction, but nonfiction and memoirs show the possibilities that Substack can provide all writers when like-minded people with similar fandoms get together to create a world-class experience for readers.

How to create a world-class Substack publication

I (Russell) read hundreds of publications every week and have kept a blog since 2010. So, I know a thing or two about the components that built this platform. I've been an online news junkie since the early days of the internet and have been reading online essays since I fell in love with Allie Brosh's *Hyperbole in a Half* (which is still the funniest thing on the internet to this day).

Not to go down a deep Allie Brosh rabbit hole, but have you read her latest book? Because I just finished reading it again. It's even funnier and more devastating the second time. If she ever comes to Substack, I will die.

I could talk about my love for Allie Brosh for way more than 10,000 words, and I might someday, but all I'm trying to do right now is establish that I am an OG blog fan. Remember webrings? Because Substack is webrings on steroids with a built-in donate button that we used to have to code ourselves.

In the 2010s, webcomics dovetailed into the rise of Kickstarter, which is where most of the weird comics I grew up reading ended up. This explains why I've backed over 700 projects on Kickstarter and fell in love with it immediately. I think Substack has an amazing opportunity to become another home for weird fiction and create a symbiotic relationship with Kickstarter to help supercharge an author's career...but that is a story for another day.

I heard about Substack for years but never really spent a ton of time here until Notes launched, and I subscribed to 100+ publications on the first day. Some people cringed when they got tons of Substack emails over the following weeks, but after that first day, I dang near cried because it captured something I thought was lost forever.

It immediately brought back memories of opening my RSS feed every morning or staying up until 2 am reading a thousand blog posts from my new favorite website.

Needless to say, I got Substack immediately in a way I haven't understood any other subscription platform. It is the closest I've ever come to reexperiencing my childhood online outside of Kickstarter.

These days, I read over 200 publications and curate a weekly digest of my favorites, so yeah, I'm a bit obsessed with the platform. When I get obsessive like this, I can literally spend hundreds of hours trying to figure out how and why something works...

...which is exactly what I did, and boy, did I learn some things.

The first thing I started to notice was that some people had these little check marks that indicated they were "bestsellers". Unlike Twitter, these badges were based on how many paid subscribers they had, which meant I suddenly had a sales metric to start studying.

Why were these bestselling publications able to scale to hundreds or thousands of members while others were struggling to get paid? Yes, some of the reason is because they owned a media company or spent years as Secretary of Labor.

Not all of them, though. ***Heck, not even more than a handful.***

It's true that many of them brought an audience outside of Substack. ***Cards on the table: I brought over 20,000 subscribers from other platforms to Substack, and they definitely helped me scale.***

I've spent a lot of time analyzing successful writers, but it's been a while since I've had a case study where I could become a guinea pig to test out what was working in real-time. The last platform I could do that with was Kickstarter, and that experience allowed me to help authors raise over $1.2 million since we launched our Kickstarter Accelerator program in January 2022.

I hope I can replicate that success here, both for myself and for some of you.

My process is the same every time I do this kind of work. First, I keep my mouth shut and study what I think is happening. Then, I find the people who seem to understand the platform best and consume everything they write about it. After that, I implement what they have said in my own practice. Finally, I share my findings with everyone else and see if they can be repeated by others.

I published my first Substack article in February 2021. I started studying the platform heavily in March 2023. I started consuming what experts had to say on the topic in April 2023 and imported all my subscribers in May 2023. Since then, I've been studying and tweaking what seems to work across hundreds of publications into my own practice. I've added my own spin from almost 30 years of consuming blogs and hosting my own for years.

I also have a degree in journalism from the University of Maryland, spent time working on Capitol Hill as a cameraman/producer, and taught media back in college.

I guess what I'm saying is that ***I know a lot about the topic of running a successful media publication*** from my own colloquial experience working in media, my experience building media companies, and my love of online media.

So, this chapter is going to dive deep into everything I've learned about building a world-class Substack publication. It's probably going to irritate a lot of people who don't want to scale their publication. So, I want to make this clear upfront...***if you are happy with where you are in the world and don't want/need help, then you should stop reading now.***

That said, I know there are a lot of people struggling to find a readership and are desperately trying to find a foothold here. ***This chapter is for them.*** If it resonates with you, awesome. Even if you only find one helpful thing, I hope it's worth it for you.

If nothing else, I'll try to make it entertaining.

This chapter will also incorporate best practices that I've found across hundreds of publications. On top of my degree in journalism, I have a degree in demographic sociology. So, my interest is mostly in how large groups of people operate. It's why I love studying audience-building and Facebook ads and enjoying exploring the nitty-gritty of how group psychology affects people.

There are literally millions of edge cases out there that don't follow any of these rules. There is nothing wrong with those publications. There are a ton of outliers here on Substack. They've specifically come here looking for a place where they could build an audience for their offbeat interests.

I have attempted to pull together as many unique and disparate threads into what I believe connect most of the successful publications on Substack, ***but most is not all.***

If you are having success, then I think that's awesome. Maybe there's something here that could make you have more success, or maybe it's all rubbish. It's possible I have discounted an entire subgenre of Substack just because I haven't found it yet. ***That was not my intention.***

This section does not attempt to capture every lived experience. It is simply a guide of what I think works most of the time based on my analysis.

One last thing: since I run a primarily nonfiction publication, I focused my examples on those types of publications. They seemed to be the ones with the most clear and immediate success path on Substack.

This is nothing against fiction on Substack. If you go to the Search tab, you can see oodles of fiction and comic publications doing stellar here. I believe that you can have success with fiction here, and there are lots of people who are very committed to making that happen.

I do think most of what I talk about below can help if you write fiction. I've helped thousands of fiction and nonfiction authors in my career. I've also written over 40 novels, produced over 1,000 comic pages, and published a ton of nonfiction.

In my experience, much, but not all, of the advice I dole out can work for both, though it needs to be modified to fit your needs. ***That is true with all advice, though.*** You dig to find the kernel of truth and then try to make it work for your business.

So, while I will attempt to use some fiction examples, I am primarily focused on nonfiction because that's what I'm trying to build here.

Defining your brand identity

There are millions of flashy logos and interesting-looking websites floating around the internet, but they are almost always hollow and unmemorable. I want to love them, but they leave me asking the same two questions: "What are you trying to say here?" and "Who are you trying to say it to?"

These are the two basic questions you must ask when building a brand, and too often, they are skipped over in favor of a flashy logo that screams nothing into the void but "Look at me, I'm pretty!"

This is antithetical to a brand's purpose. The purpose of a brand is to stand above the void and scream, "Look at me. I'm perfect for you!" It may be fun to have a cool logo, but flashy design doesn't serve the purpose of building a brand identity.

The purpose of a brand is to speak for you when you aren't there to speak for yourself. It's a reflection of you in the eyes of your ideal customers. Its job is to provide a beacon for your audience in the endless, hyper-connected fog in which we live.

Look at a company like Apple. Steve Jobs couldn't speak to every human being on the planet. He was a busy guy. Even if he could, he wouldn't be able to reach out again and again over the course of decades. He needed something that could repeatedly speak for him in the minds of the populace. Enter the Apple brand, which is possibly the greatest brand in the history of the world.

In Apple's advertising, logo, and design aesthetic, Jobs had to convey exactly what people could expect from his products without saying a single word to them. He had to create a brand so powerful that his perfect audience would rise from the endless void and hone in on his company.

This is what the right brand can do for your company. It can turn your audience building inside out and lead the right people to your door.

If you do it correctly, of course.

Generally, creatives go about building a brand too early in their company's life cycle. I know it's tough to hold off on branding since we have artistic energy brimming from every orifice, but a memorable brand isn't about artistic talent.

It's about the emotional connection with your audience.

Look at the "Life is Good" logo. There's almost no artistic talent needed to draw that stick figure, and yet it resonated with people so deeply they were able to build a company that's held up for decades.

Most creatives think a good company starts with a solid brand, but in reality, branding should be the last thing that comes about in the life cycle of a company. Until you have pinpointed your ideal customer avatar and have a complete product line aimed at them, it's useless to think about creating a brand that could change drastically with every product launch.

To fully understand your brand, you must be able to say, "This is what my company stands for," "This is who I build my products for," and "This is what I'm trying to say." This only comes with time, market research, and speaking extensively to your perfect customers.

For Wannabe Press, our history with Kickstarter made a green and yellow color scheme very appealing to me. Not only does the green stand out on marketing materials, but the coloring harkens back to our roots with grassroots fundraising.

We modeled our rebellious bee mascot off Invader Zim, a children's cartoon created by Jhonen Vasquez. He was a huge influence on me and an even bigger influence on my audience. Once we figured that out, it was a no-brainer to use Invader Zim as the basis for our logo. We filled her with attitude because that rebellious spirit embodied everything we knew about our ideal customers.

We didn't start with our mascot, though. We only designed it after years of building our audience. It was borne out of seeing how people reacted to our products. It came from watching who bought our books again and again. It was a reflection of what we saw in the people who liked our products. We weren't trying to stuff a mascot down our audience's throats. We saw what they responded to and made something that spoke to them.

That's the true secret to building a memorable brand. You build it as you go until it reflects your ideal client perfectly. They tell you exactly what they want, and then you mirror it back to them. Once you can do that, your brand will stick out like a beacon in the endless void.

"Brand identity" elicits groans from most authors I talk to, but a brand is nothing more than the promise you make to your readers that allows them to fall in love with your work.

Some authors have a very tight topic they write about, like Anne Rice. I know exactly what emotion I will get from her work every single time. Other authors, like David Sedaris, talk about a wide range of topics and I follow him for the unique way he looks at a wide range of topics.

Both of these authors have a great brand and a strong voice, but they go about defining their brands in very different ways.

I mean, can't you close your eyes and picture David Sedaris's voice in your head? It's wry, dry, and snarky, with a heavy dose of pathos that allows him to connect deeply with even the most mundane topics.

Now, do the same thing and picture Anne Rice. She hasn't spent nearly as much time on stage as David Sedaris, but can't you picture a hauntingly beautiful love story between monstrous people played out over countless tragedies in an endless existence?

That voice you hear is their brand. It's the first step to defining your publication. I started developing The Author Stack around a topic I saw pop up in a Convertkit email about their Craft + Commerce conference. After that email, I started seeing people "sitting at the intersection of craft and commerce" all over the place.

I've had a ton of trouble defining my nonfiction brand in the past because I like to talk about a wide-ranging set of issues, from how to write great books to how to make more money selling them.

As such, I kind of fell outside the norm when it came to branding myself. I wasn't a craft person, but I also wasn't a salesperson. I really dealt with this small piece of the process that revolved around how to marry craft and commerce so you could build a career without feeling like you were selling your soul to do it.

When I saw that hook starting to circulate, I knew I had found my brand. In fact, I had always had that brand, because my voice has been the same for a long time, but now I had the language to define that brand.

Since I developed that language and married it to my existing voice, I have been able to scale way better than I ever have before. Why? Because people can now hit my publication and, in one sentence, understand my value proposition and unique selling point.

People aren't going to buy from you just because you're awesome. Well, at least it's not only because you are awesome. It's because of two factors: The Value Proposition of what you have to offer and the Unique Selling Point that sets you apart.

The Value Proposition is the tangible result somebody will get from buying your product. When you are selling a solution, this can be something like "lose sixty pounds in twenty days" or "build your retirement funds from zero to a million dollars in the next year". These are value propositions that are easy and tangible to understand. If you buy that product, you will see measurable changes in your life.

With a creative product, value is harder to determine. It deals much more with the emotional attachment a buyer has to your product than with its tangible benefit. The value they might see is meeting an artist in person and having them sign their work. The subject matter of your work might resonate with them, or it might be the fact they are getting a handmade, completely original piece of art. These are all ways to emotionally resonate with your client, and every client will resonate with different products for different reasons.

However, there are tangible value propositions you can offer with creative products, too. For instance, cutting the cost of your product by 25 percent makes people believe they are getting a better deal. Additionally, offering a 2-for-1 discount is another way to give tangible value to a product. Even if you plan on selling a product for three dollars, it is better to price it at five dollars so you can discount it down to three. People see the value in something as originally priced and are always after a deal.

JCPenney used this strategy for years. They priced their product higher than their intended selling price so they could mark it down and show people they were getting value. They changed this policy for a short while and made their pricing more transparent. Customers hated this change, and sales plummeted because, in the buyer's mind, they weren't getting as good a deal as before. It was a disaster for JCPenney, but it shows how powerful the idea of a discount really is and how a company can misalign itself with the value proposition of its customers.

When deciding on your value proposition, it's important to understand not all buyers will resonate with your value proposition. That's okay. Your job is not to attract all buyers. It's to attract the right ones for your offer.

Because of this, it's critically important to ask yourself what the value proposition is that you are offering to your potential clients. Is your value based on the lowest price, the best customer service, the highest quality, or some other factor?

If you can narrow this down, it will help define your pitch to potential clients and justify the price you charge. Additionally, it will help determine where you stand in the market and how much your product should cost to make.

A Unique Selling Point is simply what makes your product one of a kind. The unique selling point sets you apart from every other creative on the planet. It's something only you have.

When somebody comes to your store, they have the choice of thousands, if not millions, of creatives. Your job is to figure out how you are different and why somebody should buy from you. It's not the buyer's job to decide to buy from you; it's your job to convince the buyer you are the right fit for them.

Your unique selling point might be that you print all your artwork in a certain way or that you use certain materials. It might have to do with your worldview, the types of products you make, or the subject matter of your artwork. The unique selling point is something nobody else has except for you.

My friend Leen Isabel makes a comic book about pole dancing. While the book is great, the unique selling point is that it's the only comic book I've ever seen about pole dancing that is made for female pole dancers instead of oversexualized boys. That unique hook resonates with her intended audience. Pole Dancing Adventure isn't for everybody, but its unique selling point makes the right person immediately attracted to her book.

If you can determine the value proposition and unique selling point in your work, you will be on the path toward figuring out everything else related to your business. It will give you a direction for your branding, your ideal customer, and everything else that we talk about for the rest of this book.

So, what is your value proposition? Where do you stand in the market? Are you more concerned with the quality or quantity of sales? What do you want to convey to your customers about the value of your product? What separates you from the rest of your competition? Why are you unique?

If you can answer those questions, you will be well on your way to building your career. If you can't, then this is the time to start thinking about it! Jot down some notes and ask a trusted friend or critic.

What's really important to note here is that building your brand should not be about changing your writing to fit some predefined mold. It is about finding the language to define what you offer readers in a clear and concise manner.

A great exercise to help with this is the 7-word bio. Can you define your brand in seven words? Mine is ***I help authors build better businesses.***

***

With Sparkle*—mine is "I help folks stay creative on Substack."*

***

How do you relate to readers?

Are you relatable, educational, inspirational, or aspirational? It seems like successful nonfiction Substack publications focus on one of four areas.

There are those who **seek to educate or report,** those who seek to **relate to others** and make them feel seen, those who seek to **inspire people into action**, and those who seek to **create an aspirational path** for people to strive to achieve.

Educators inform on a topic. Realtors meet people where they are and show them they are not alone. Inspirers plant a spark to spur people into action. Aspirers show people how to become their best selves.

I've seen this across niches on Substack, and while every blog contains multitudes, it seems like blogs, by and large, choose one of these paths when they want to scale.

There are a lot of people who use Substack to gather information and disseminate it. There is no call to action or desire to spark action. They are there to educate, and I think this is a bedrock foundation of online blogs since the beginning of the internet. A ton of aspiring nonfiction authors take this tactic to build authority before they develop their own processes.

Whereas somebody who is there for relatability... I think of somebody like Jenny Lawson, Allie Brosh, or David Sedaris. They are not there to ignite action. They are there to shine a light up to the world and say, "Isn't this experience super relatable? You are not alone if you feel this way."

As opposed to somebody who is there to ignite action...those are people who are there to poke somebody into realizing they want a change or inspire them to take action...but they are not going to tell them exactly how to do that or give step-by-step instructions.

Whereas somebody who is there for aspiration is there to actually say, "You have been inspired; now let me show you how to get there."

Those are the four main ways successful publications go about using a substack.

For instance, Monica calls herself the author analyst. Her job, I think she would say this, too, is to understand the scope of a situation and show you the good and the bad of it from her point of view.

Whereas, by the time you get to me, you kind of already know there's a problem and are inspired to fix it. So, I live on the other end of that spectrum.

When somebody wants step-by-step on how to set up sections, how to build a virtual summit, or whatever is blocking them from success, they come to me because I will show them exactly how to do it, but I care less about getting you to understand the scope of the problem.

Monica also does the aspirational stuff because she literally has books with how-tos and step-by-step instructions on all manner of publishing topics. However, for her Substack specifically, she's found a more reporterly lane. Meanwhile, I have taken the expert track with mine.

I think we both attract similar audiences, which is why we work well together, but on Substack, we do different things. A good publication has all of these components to it, but it specializes in one above the others.

One of the biggest questions I get asked about this is ***how to tell the difference between an inspirational blog and an aspirational one.*** I would differentiate them by asking the following question:

Are you looking to make the lightbulb go off in somebody's head and inspire them to take action, or are you more interested in showing them how to grow with action?

Upworthy is inspirational. *Chicken Soup for the Soul* is inspirational. They fill you with hope that things could change, but they don't tell you how to make that change.

The Four-Hour Work Week is aspirational. It takes that inspiration and puts it into action. It's the tactical and practical that takes the inspirational and makes it actionable.

It's a small distinction but an important one. Not everyone who wants to be inspired is ready to grow, and while you can do both, the ones who choose one or the other consistently seem better able to scale.

Defining your voice

One of the best resources for defining your voice and the direction of your publication is *7 Figure Fiction*, specifically Theodora Taylor's idea of universal fantasies.

Oh, you don't know about universal fantasies? Read *7 Figure Fiction* right now.

No, this isn't just for fantasy authors. It's for EVERY author, no matter what you write (even if you write nonfiction).

Do not write another book without absorbing it into your bones.

It's probably the most crucial piece of book marketing in the last year, aside from my books with Monica and our solo books, of course.

But honestly, it might be more important because our books discuss how you can make sales and the levers you can pull, but that book gets to the core of why good book marketing works.

It basically boils down to this: what escapist fantasies are readers getting from your work? What singular need in the reader's psyche are you fulfilling with your fiction?

Mine is easy. It's empowerment.

For years, people have told me they love my work because the characters have agency in a cruel world, and they use that agency to affect change.

It might seem obvious to me now, but it wasn't until I read that book it all clicked, and I turned my marketing toward that aim: finding people who wanted fantasy that empowers them.

Not only that, but it is a guide for every book I write. Does it deliver on that Universal Fantasy or not?

Using that one phrase, I can very easily tailor ALL my messaging to that end and drill down on the fact that the thing you will get out of my work is a feeling of agency in a chaotic world.

Bad guys are beaten. Good guys win. The cruel world is bent to the will of justice. It's noblebright fantasy; I just didn't know it then.

There are all sorts of universal fantasies out there (which is why you should read the book), but you need to figure out YOURS.

For years, I have told people all sorts of things to get started, but now I tell authors one thing when it comes to marketing.

What is the Universal Fantasy that your work fulfills?

This can be different per series, but generally, once you have a couple of series, you will find that the UF of your series is pretty consistent because it's at the core of all your work.

If a long-time fan doesn't like one of your books, especially if you have a wide catalog, it's probably because you didn't deliver the universal fantasy you are known for as an author.

Once you have that piece and figure out what people will GAIN from reading your work, you are on the path to showing them why they should care about your work because you are finally answering the most important question in marketing.

What's in it for ***THEM?***

Mine is empowerment. With every article and post, I try to make you feel like you have control, or can get in control, of your career.

While every successful publication will have some of each, successful authors generally rely on one universal fantasy to drive their work. It is that singular fantasy that brings people coming back for more of their work.

Every Substack will have multiple types of posts inside of it, but when somebody finds your publication, they need to know what to expect from your brand immediately. The quicker they can know that, the better.

I read Tara McMullin for a different reason than I read other publications, but I know the general vibe of their content and what they are going to evoke in me with each piece they write.

When I go to share their publication with others, I know why I should share it and with whom. I know what headspace I need to be in to get the most from either.

I know I will be telling the same stories for the same audience for years because even when I'm not being paid, that's what I like talking about and thinking about, the same sort of things in the same sort of ways.

Marketing is just the thing you do consistently positioned in such a way that people who resonate with what you can do can find you easily and know they are in the right place quickly.

Some people get that right the first time, and others have to build up and burn down their work lots of times to figure it out. I am one of the latter.

People often push back on my Substack advice, telling me that the only reason I am having success with Substack is because I am a USA Today Bestselling author or because I've had a long, distinguished career.

Of course, they discount all the myriad of failures I've had building successful memberships and blogs over the years because it doesn't fit neatly into that narrative.

Having a long career is just one more thing I can point out to help new readers grow to trust my work quickly. The quicker somebody can land on my publication and know it's something they will love, the easier it will be to convert them into a subscriber.

When I started my Substack and decided to go all in on it, I asked what the maximum value I could provide to people was so they could say it was worth it.

I decided that if somebody could look at the free courses they got for enrolling and the dozen+ books I had available to them and still say no, then I had done all I could.

I started doing this work in 2004 and didn't have any real success until 2017. Even then, it took until 2021 for me to start having any real nonfiction success.

So, I am fully aware of how hard it is to scale. However, there are things you can do for cheap or free to help you get there faster, like utilizing psychological triggers in your work to help influence reader buying decisions.

Psychological triggers convince people to trust faster and fall deeper in love with your work. There are a ton of these, but *How to Build a Creative Career* talks about the big six:

Commitment—When somebody willingly commits to joining your community, they are more likely to buy your product. This is the main value to people joining your mailing list, wearing a button, or even taking a flier. They make a commitment when performing that action. It signifies they are part of your community. The more actions they take, the more commitment they build.

Every time they open a newsletter from you and don't unsubscribe, they are affirming that commitment. Every time they like one of your tweets or share a Facebook post, they are affirming their commitment to your brand again and again. The more you can enforce that commitment through words and actions, the more likely you are to have an enthusiastic ambassador for your brand—one who buys all your stuff.

Reciprocity—When you do something nice for somebody, they want to help you. That's just human nature. Knowing this, you need to provide value for your potential customer before you ever ask for a sale. Once you have provided incredible value through advice or some free content, then people will gladly give you money because you have helped them and treated them like human beings.

Social Proof—Human beings want to be part of the "in" crowd. If you can prove that other people are using your product, everybody else will want to use it, too. The hardest sales to make at conventions are the first ones. Once people are running around the show floor with your product, other people are more likely to want it, as well.

Your work becomes valuable to a customer because other people see the value in it already. People want to buy what their peers buy. They don't want to be left out in the cold. If you can show your customers that people they like and respect use your product, then you are more likely to convince them to buy it, too.

Scarcity—When you limit the available quantity of a product, customers become increasingly likely to make a buying decision. People believe products will be around forever and that they can always buy them later. When they realize a product is in limited supply, they are forced to make an immediate decision. This works wonders for people sitting on the fence about buying your product and also for people who desperately want your product but need a little push to take action.

Authority—If you can demonstrate that you are an expert in your field, people are more likely to buy your product over somebody else's. This is how you stand out above every other creative who is doing exactly what you do. They choose you because you are an expert in your field.

To prove your expertise, it's important to have consistently high-selling products for a long time, and it helps if you're able to teach other people how to do what you do. Another way is to write guest posts on other blogs, share your work on podcasts, or speak on panels. You can also use platforms like Medium and Kickstarter to build expertise, as the platform's authority can be transferred to you.

Liking—If somebody has a positive connection to you, they are more likely to buy from you. Think about it: You are more inclined to buy from somebody you like than somebody you don't care about, right? Of course, you are.

Each of those triggers reinforces people's ability to trust faster. The more of these you use, the faster and deeper that connection becomes over time. These triggers stack on top of each other and compound to help you find the right readers more quickly with each post you make.

Yes, the USA Today bestselling author is one thing, as is the long-term success, but they are all just little triggers to indicate you should pay attention, and then I deliver on that.

Success comes from having all of these things reinforce and amplify each other.

I still have to go out and do the hard work of getting people to pay attention every day and then retain that attention.

What goes into creating your voice?

All this is fine and good, but what actually goes into creating your voice? Well, I'm a bit of a huge data nerd so I have a quantifiable data nerd answer for you. As I see it, it comes down to a couple of principles working in congress with each other.

1. What is your universal fantasy?
2. What are the psychological triggers that inform that fantasy with your audience?
3. What are the tropes that inform those psychological triggers in your genre?
4. What recurring themes in your work reinforce those tropes?
5. What lived experiences/traumas inform those themes?
6. What prose styles reinforce those lived experiences?

Mix those all up in a blender and layer them on top of each other like Swiss cheese. Then, make it your own as your writing evolves with time, and those are the main factors I see in an author's voice.

I can say that my work, both fiction and nonfiction, is about giving the reader agency in a world that seems intent to take it away. It's all about empowerment because that's my universal fantasy.

I'm trying to make you understand that ***you are the hero of your own story***, so my writing tends to be terse, to the point, and filled with actionable steps that are easy to follow. I don't use a lot of flowery language because I don't want you to get lost in the pretty words.

I want to deliver a gut punch that gets you off the couch and gives you the tools to change your own life for the better. I don't want my message to get lost in the language, so I usually keep it plain.

My work, both fiction and nonfiction, is also aspirational. It's about how you can become the you that you always thought you could be.

I tend to write in genres that encourage that relationship, and the trope I use most of the time is the Chosen One narrative. That is what has mostly consumed my career.

I deliver the same type of experience whether I'm writing fiction or nonfiction. It's always always always about you; a regular human can rise and take control of their destiny.

Creating a branding document

By now, you should have a good idea of your brand and the type of experience you want to curate. We have spent thousands of words getting the basic concept of your publication rock solid so that we can create a branding document and get all the resources in place for your publication to feel like a singular and cohesive experience.

Now, it's time to start building the elements of your page to fit your specific aesthetic. The first thing you want to do is to create a lookbook of publications that resonate with you.

First and foremost, we've got to start with just what, exactly, is a brand lookbook. In essence, these are collections of photographs or images that have been compiled to show off your brand by highlighting its products, services, designs, or other work.

Brand lookbooks are integral for introducing new and prospective clients and customers to your company and what it does, and they help by setting the tone for every subsequent interaction.

The word lookbook might induce more groans, but the work of creating a lookbook is super fun. It basically involves diving down rabbit holes of your favorite things and putting them together in a folder on your computer so you can reference them.

The best way to do this on Substack is to start with the publications you have already read and click through them all to see which homepages make you feel good. Some of them will elicit no reaction, but you'll immediately feel like others call out to you. When you find those, screenshot them and stuff them in a folder. Then, take the URL and make a text document where you can collate them all.

I should note that you may resonate with publications that are different from the one you are making. If that happens, I would first question whether you are really making the right publication for yourself. If you continue to move forward, then I would focus on publications that target the same types of readers that you want to follow your publication and develop your universal fantasy for them.

A good rule is that ***if you can't immediately tell what a publication is going for or who they are targeting, then you probably don't want to use them as an example.***

Once you go through the publications you have already read, it's time to expand into other publications. There are a couple of ways to do this for maximum impact.

- See if that publication is recommending any other publications. It's a good bet that a publication is recommending other Substacks they think their audience would grok.

- Go to the publication owner's page and see what they are reading. For the same reason as the above, it's a good bet at least some of those publications are ones that you should be checking out.

- On the same page, look at the notes they are sharing and check out those publications. Additionally, see who is commenting on those notes and check out those publications as well.

If you were wondering about how I could follow so many publications, this is why. If I think something is even moderately interesting, I will subscribe to the publication and check it out later. If even 10% of them show me one thing that helps me, it's worth it for me to stay subscribed.

Make sure to take note of the types of imagery they use, the headlines they tend to share, how often they post, and the length of their articles, as this will also help build the basis for your articles as well.

For instance, I started to notice some of my favorite publications either were a digest of the most interesting articles around or built a digest of their favorite articles into their publication.

I hadn't done a digest in a long while, but I used to follow Tim Ferris's Five Bullet Friday as a template for years with my own newsletter and knew subscribers loved it, so I knew how to make a digest. Since I already read so many publications, it became easy to add one every weekend. I took note of when most of the digests came out (Sunday) and tried to find a day that allowed mine to stand out a bit, which is why I share mine on Saturday.

I spend a lot of time modeling other successful publications, but I think it's invaluable.

Most creative professionals don't like sales and marketing because it feels too much like begging. People hate to beg. I hate to beg, too. I don't think anybody likes to beg; however, sales isn't about begging.

Do you ever think Starbucks begs for your money? Does it ever feel like begging when they post a billboard or run a TV spot?

Of course not. That would be crazy. Their marketing isn't begging, is it?

You bet it is. Every time they run an ad, they are saying, "Please come buy our coffee because if you don't, we'll go bankrupt." Every time you see one of their billboards, they are pleading with you to spend just one dollar with them so they don't have to shut down their storefronts.

They aren't running those ads for the heck of it. They are running ads because they know begging for your money is essential to making their business successful. Starbucks spends millions of dollars a year begging for your money.

It never comes across as begging, though, does it? I've never once looked at a Starbucks ad and thought, "Wow. They must be desperate for my money."

And that's because Starbucks doesn't see it as begging. They see it as effective marketing. Effective marketing brings more money through the doors. They don't position their marketing as begging, so it doesn't come across as begging. They position their marketing as showing off their awesome stuff in the best light possible.

This is an important mindset shift you must employ to be successful as a creative professional. You must use marketing effectively, like Starbucks. But once we get over that mental block, how can we compete with a company like Starbucks, whose marketing budget is astronomical?

That's the easy part. Starbucks is everywhere; their marketing is ubiquitous. While they won't ever tell you specific sales figures on a product, you can gauge effective marketing by how long a campaign runs and whether a product stays on their menu. Something like their pumpkin spice latte has very effective marketing.

The same is true in creative fields. Whether it's graphic design or publishing, there are billion-dollar players in your space spending millions of dollars on marketing every year. By studying them, you can model their success in your own business.

If you are a freelancer, there are individual creators who market themselves to acquire new business, as well. You can model their success just as easily as you can model the success of a company. All you have to do is follow their career and study their habits.

If you are trying to sell more prints at shows, look through the art books of successful show artists and mimic their price points. If you are a writer, study successful authors in your genre and find out what makes them special. If you want your work hung in a gallery, you can meet with fine artists to discover their process for getting a dealer.

All of this research is easily accomplished with a few days of studying. This isn't stealing, mind you. You aren't going to copy anything directly. You are simply getting a feel for how a successful person or company runs their business and then modeling their success in your own life.

This includes being on the same social media platforms, targeting the same users, and using similar color patterns in your logo to maximize your chances for success. Your goal is to take their accomplishments (and their failures) and use them to quickly catapult your business beyond what you could do alone. If the average path to success takes ten years, you might be able to do it in eight or even six if you model success effectively.

If you aren't modeling success, then you are setting yourself up for failure. You will have to spend millions of dollars that you don't have on your own research. Then, you'll have to put brand-new products on the market and play catch-up with those same companies that are already positioned better than you in the marketplace. It's a recipe for disaster.

By modeling successful players in your industry, you can move yourself ahead drastically with none of the upfront cost and very little time investment.

Additionally, if you model success, you will begin to feel successful. The more success builds in your company, the more confident you will be in your own life...leading to more success.

Please note I am not talking about stealing what other people are doing verbatim. I am saying that if other people have already found success doing it, and especially if you see dozens of publications doing it, then there's a good chance you might have success with it, too.

However, you still need to put your own spin on it. With so many options available, this kind of strategy can help you show what is working now. Additionally, by subscribing to these publications, you'll be able to see changes you need to be aware of regarding how you should conduct your own business.

On top of all that, by analyzing a bunch of publications to construct your lookbook, you'll likely see something they are obviously doing wrong that can become the unique selling proposition of your own publication.

In fiction, we call that subverting the trope. I do it a ton in my work, especially with the Chosen One narrative, but it only works if you know everything about that trope and twist it with reverence instead of malice. There are several publications like

Valerie Monroe's *How Not to F*** Up Your Face* or Jessica DeFino's *The Unpublishable* that take the existing model of beauty journalism and upend them.

However, it only works so well because they clearly love that kind of journalism and they are speaking to the deep core of something the audience knows already and isn't getting from mainstream publications. Without that deep-seated knowledge of the industry at large, the same publication would feel flat and uninteresting, or worse, a parody that would alienate the reader instead of bringing them into a shared joke.

Once you have worked through all the Substacks that seem relevant, expand out to other publications and even other media, especially to find colors that really speak to you. However, they will likely be less relevant because they have more flexibility with how they set up their site.

For instance, I Love Big Magic by Elizabeth Gilbert. You can likely see the massive influence the original cover for that book had on my brand here.

A lookbook could probably just as easily be called a vibe book because what you're really trying to do is figure out the vibes that speak to you and speak to your audience. Your brand sits right in the middle where those two things intersect.

Bringing the brand together

Now that you have your lookbook together, it's time to get the elements of your brand in place. We aren't going to put it on your site yet, but we need a logo and a wordmark to get started.

Here is a quick image dimension key that Substack uses for its graphics.

Image dimension key.

- Logo: At least 256 x 256 pixels, with a transparent background.
- Wordmark: At least 1,344 x 256 pixels, with a maximum aspect ratio of 21:4.
- Cover photo: At least 600 x 600 pixels.
- Social/post preview image: We recommend at least 1,456 x 1,048 pixels, but 420 x 300 is the minimum. 14:10 is the aspect ratio for the preview images. -Substack.

I would recommend doing a logo of at least 1000x1000 because, in this instance, size does matter.

How do you find your logo? Well, if you're still having trouble picturing what you want, then there are a couple of ways that you can get clarity.

- Sara Tasker - Me & Orla and Keeley Rees offer this amazing Substack branding bundle to free subscribers to their publication, *The Substack Soirée,* to help put together an amazing brand.
- Hire a graphic designer. I keep a running recommendations list on my author website, but you can also look at hiring somebody on Fiverr or Upwork.
- There are still a lot of moral and ethical question marks when it comes to using AI to produce imagery, and I certainly would

never use it for something as important as a logo. However, you might consider using Midjourney or Dall-E to get the vibes of your logo.

- My new favorite method is to use DepositPhotos and search for vector-only imagery. They have some great, high-end options that come royalty-free, and they provide a commercial license for a reasonable fee. If you're looking for a deal, then about four times a year, Appsumo runs a discount on DepositPhotos, where you can get 100 images for $30. It's worth waiting for that if you can wait. Plus, then you can use it to get even more imagery for your posts and preview imagery. What happens if somebody else uses your image? ***I guess that's why I have hundreds of images, so I can find a new one.***

Once you have your logo, you need to work on your wordmark. This is basically just the title of your publication. You can make it using Canva, GIMP, Affinity, Adobe, or any number of image manipulation tools. I used Coolvetica for mine because I believe everything is cooler with Helvetica.

If you're having trouble finding a great font, I recommend DaFont, Blambot, Comicraft, or 1001fonts to find something that matches your brand. Once you have those, head to DASHBOARD>SETTINGS>BASIC and plug them into your site.

Before we talk about a few final bits, we should talk about your title. The title of your publication is the first brand interaction most people will have with your brand, so you want to make it count. I chose Author Stack because I assumed there would eventually be a #authorstack hashtag similar to TikTok and Twitter. I thought it would be good SEO to have a very searchable title that authors would likely look up often.

Authors usually groan at hearing the term SEO, but for our purposes, what is most important is to pick something that your ideal reader will resonate with immediately when they see the headline. I think a better term for SEO is "seek-engine optimization", which means that when people seek out your advice, they can find you easily and know they are in the right place.

If you already have a title cooking, then great. However, if you are looking for inspiration, you should check out Google Trends and try to find words in your category that people often search for. It's free and easy(ish) to use.

Ideally, you are looking for something that has been highly searchable for a long time. Since you're going to (hopefully) have this publication for years, I would still always choose a word that is less popular but has longevity than one that has been more popular for a shorter time.

The only exception I would make to that is if a new technology or trend like TikTok came onto the market and the terms didn't even exist or had much lower relevance before the platform existed, but now it has staying power.

Your About page

Now that we've plugged in the title and main imagery of your site, it's time to talk about your About page. Aside from your homepage, this will likely be the most visited page of your whole site, and it needs to tell people exactly what they are getting as quickly as possible. Even if you have a meandering brand that touches on many things, people need to know that upfront.

This is also the page others will look at for cross-collaborations and to hype up your brand, so it's good to have everything they need high enough that they don't have to scroll. For mine, I put the cover image at the top of the page, and then here is my first paragraph:

Welcome to the Author Stack. *This publication sits at the intersection of craft and commerce, helping writers build more sustainable businesses that allow them to thrive while creating work that lights them up inside.* ***We strive to give authors agency in a world that too often seems intent on stripping it away from them.***

Notice how I state the name of the publication and then tell people exactly what to expect. I also added a slightly modified 7-word pitch (***helping writers build more sustainable businesses***) and ended with my universal fantasy. It's all there in less than 100 words.

After that, I added my bio and expanded on why you should trust me to lead you on this journey. I focused on my value proposition and unique selling proposition throughout, with each paragraph going deeper and deeper into why somebody should trust me. Because my publication is about giving you agency, I decided to end with a positive message about the future to demonstrate the hopeful nature of my articles.

If you have specific days of the week you publish or special perks for paid subscribers, this is a good place to lay them out. However, the most important thing is to keep people excited about the possibilities and not weigh them down with extraneous information. ***Your job is to sell them on why they should subscribe, and once you have sold them, stop selling.***

I won't tell you the exact length, but I will say that every paragraph should reinforce the central thesis of why somebody should subscribe to hear more about your work.

Now, it's time to condense this to your short description, which has, as of yet, been empty. You can find the short description under the Publication name in DASHBOARD>SETTINGS>BASICS.

The reason we did the About page before the short description is that they should inform each other. By far, the most read part of your publication will be the short description, but that will be reinforced by your About page and homepage. Most writers find it easier to write a short description after the About page, but if you want to write your short description first, do you, honey boo-boo.

Mine is one sentence that sums up my whole About page.

Helping create a sustainable path forward for authors to build businesses that allow them to thrive and lives that light them up inside.

You can see that while this isn't exactly like the first paragraph of my About page, it's close. You can probably get away with just copying the first paragraph of your About page here, but you might want to make it punchier and give it a better hook.

Once you've got that sorted, let's scroll down to DASHBOARD>SETTINGS>PUBLICATION DETAILS and click EDIT next to the EMAIL, BANNER, HEADER, and FOOTER SETTINGS.

It is best practice to create a header for your emails that reintroduces you to readers with every email you send them. People are busy and may not remember you between signing up and your first few emails, so it's always good to give them a nice reminder.

Luckily, this looks a lot like the short description and About page you've already made. Here is mine.

Hi, I'm USA Today bestselling fantasy author, editor, and publisher Russell Nohelty. I sit at the intersection of craft and commerce, helping writers navigate the sticky bit between writing something that lights them up inside and building an audience of superfans who adore their work.

Notice, this is close to the exact wording of what they'll most likely read to get themselves subscribed in the first place. Additionally, you should change your profile page to mimic this imagery so that if people find you on chat, threads, or notes, they will know what you are all about quickly.

This is my profile bio:

USA Today bestselling author of fantasy books and comics who sits at the intersection of craft and commerce, helping authors create sustainable businesses that light them up inside.

Once you have all this work, it should be a simple matter to scroll to DASHBOARD>SETTINGS>BASIC and EDIT the WELCOME EMAILS to your free and paid subscribers.

The stock emails are fine, but this is the first email anyone will get from your publication, so it is your chance to make it your own. It's a good idea to add a picture of yourself if you are comfortable doing so, as it will help people trust you.

I like to tell new readers all about the bonus courses and sections available to paid members to encourage them to sign up for a paid subscription.

Turning your About page into a hero post

One of the recent big trends on Substack is turning your About page into a hero post. Hero posts started to gain traction late in 2023 as a way to provide new subscribers with a guide to your publication. Since Substack does not allow automation sequences, you need some way to get people excited to read your articles. The solution of note has become the hero post.

There are infinite ways to create a hero post, but the easiest one is to add links to your articles under what you've already created on your About page. On my hero post, which I've titled START HERE and pinned to the top of my publication, I created several sections of my work so people can find what they are looking for at the time.

It's as easy to create a list of your articles as copying and pasting links into your post editor. When you paste a link into the editor, it should pull in the featured image, title, and more so that it looks pretty. There are two caveats here.

It took me forever to learn this, but if you hover over the imported information, three lines should appear on the right. If you click that, you should be able to choose either a small, medium, or large image. Since you'll be listing a bunch of things there, I recommend the small display. You can also convert it to a link if you prefer.

The second thing is that this will only pull in the featured image on YOUR publication. If you pull from another publication, it won't pull in the image, and you can't change the display, which is frustrating. If you have a lot of articles on other publications, like I do, you might want to consider just making a list of those and hyperlinking text instead of going through this process.

This page should be a one-stop shop for people to learn about you and your publication. So, make it thorough and engaging. If you only have a couple of articles, or you don't have any, then you don't have to worry about this yet but make a note to come back in six months and beef it up then. You might even be ready to write a table of contents, too.

Once you're done, make sure you go to the post, click the three dots on the far right side, and click PIN TO HOMEPAGE so it shows up first thing when people get to your page.

Picking your categories

Now, it's time to pick your categories. Which category is best for you? Well, by now, you should absolutely know that because you've dug deep into your brand. However, if you're not quite sure, go to each category in the Search tab, find your model publications, and then follow whatever category they are in because it's likely their fans will be searching for you.

The Search tab is the best reason to be tactical in your choices. If you look through the category, you can see what other publications I think will resonate with my readers.

This goes back to the seek-engine optimization. Your goal should be to be where the people who want to hear your message are, then make it very easy for them to find you by waving a big flag showing how you will be a great fit into their existing ecosystem.

Additionally, when you are in the right category and attracting the right audience, then other writers in your category will be excited to network and work with you. If you are having trouble finding your network of other writers, it's a pretty good bet that your brand needs better alignment.

The more ways you can align your brand, the better. I also have a profile picture that mimics my logo in color and style. I want somebody to see my image, get interested, read the bio, get more interested, and keep falling deeper and deeper down the rabbit hole into my publication.

Every time you break that immersion, you decrease how many people who find your work will resonate with it.

If you've been reading along all this way, then hopefully, you have started to see that nothing about this is the scammy marketing most authors have been taught. Instead, it's the kind of brand alignment that hopefully resonates with you because it's all about being findable to the people you want to serve.

When you are in alignment, then you maximize your chances of finding the people you're meant to serve. Additionally, if you are exhausted with marketing, these are the kinds of changes you can make once and more than double conversions, meaning more people who hit your homepage will convert into readers, who will convert into subscribers, who will convert into members.

This is the kind of work you need to do once, and it keeps feeding you forever. It's only when it stops working that you need to go back and think about refreshing your brand, but years could separate them. Meanwhile, every piece of marketing you do will be more effective once you do this work.

***

With Sparkle—I played around to see how moving categories fuelled new subscribers. I settled in education because it's a 'quieter' category than Culture, and it means I have a top 15 publication.

Wellbeing enthusiast Kate Eskuri has 1000s of paid subscribers and is in the top 10 of all publications in *Health and Wellness*. She sent me her insight;

"While I firmly believe that a writer's sense of accomplishment shouldn't hinge solely on their leaderboard position, the first time I realized my 'ranking' had a profound effect on me. I never anticipated breaking into the top 100, yet there I stood, in 22nd place!

It was a moment that genuinely brought tears to my eyes and served as a catalyst for continued growth.

In the realm of online platforms, it's all too easy to succumb to imposter syndrome.

However, seeing my name listed alongside other writers and creators whom I admire served as a powerful validation that I was indeed on the right path.

That said, it's NOT everything.

Since that initial surge of encouragement, I've consciously taken a step back from the leaderboard to avoid becoming obsessive. I now check it approximately once a month, using it primarily as a metric to gauge performance—has my ranking gone up? Down?

Is there anything that I could attribute those trends to? It's like a bit of a performance review and opportunity for reflection!"

Notes Daily Top 5s

You might have seen some of the 'Top 5' lists in Notes...those seem to be daily lists, and the leaderboards are slightly different.

For example, your publication could be 'top 3' in Parenting today but still only 'top 50' on the Explore page leaderboard.

It looks like you *might* have to have paid subscriptions turned on to make it onto the Explore page leaderboards, but you can make it onto the dailies and get lots of eyes on your work that way.

Here's another take on it

Lucy Werner, a PR consultant from Hype Yourself and a top 50 publication in the Business category, said:

"I deliberately put myself in business, which I was told is a highly competitive category, because I like to set audacious goals for myself. Whether that's my own small business book or Substack. If I can disrupt a list of predominantly men, that's great. At my last count, I was one of 23 women in the Top 50 for business.

Unlike many other business publications, I also talk about personal life. For me, the ultimate business success as an entrepreneur is to have a lovely life supported by my business. The small business and freelance economy is still growing, and the reality is that for many of us, it's to fit around our personal lives. I want to try to showcase this to these people, too.

It's nice to have for social proof, but I'm not losing sleep about it. My success on Substack isn't governed by being invited to their parties, having them recommend me or hitting a certain place on a list.

In fact, how much more fun would it be if I smashed it without them endorsing me? I'm sort of more confident in it being the latter happening anyway."

Sub-bot (Substack's inbuilt AI bot) had advice for us, too

1. Focus on growing both your free and paid subscribers, as the number of subscribers is a key factor in rankings.

2. Engage with your readers and encourage them to share your Substack with others. This can help increase your subscriber count.

3. Utilize Substack's cross-promotion tools, like Recommendations, to get endorsed by other writers, which can help you gain new subscribers (read more).

4. Make sure you're posting regularly and creating content that resonates with your audience, as engagement can influence your visibility on the platform.

***

Customizing your homepage

It might seem like we did a lot of work before customizing your homepage, but it's going to make this step so much easier. For instance, the short description we wrote shows up in the sidebar of your publication if you use the subscribe widget during your design.

To customize your homepage, go to SETTINGS>BASICS>SITE DESIGN>CUSTOMIZE

From there, you'll be able to customize the branding, including logos and wordmark, background color, accent color, and fonts for your site. In web design, we call these "global settings" because they remain consistent for your whole publication.

I highly recommend a white background because it gives the best contrast, but many successful publications made different choices. I personally would rather die than have a non-white background for my site (saving dark mode for night reading).

The biggest thing to note here is that your accent color is the color that will show up as your button color and hyperlink color.

While you can choose any HEX color for your publication, you are offered 27 "preferred" choices. Against the default white background, only 6 of these colors fall into the recommended minimum 4.5:1 contrast ratio recommended for web accessibility, and one of those is black.

- **#5365D0** - 5.07
- **#7756E3** - 4.97
- **#226216** - 7.43
- **#554615** - 9.24
- **#7E2310** - 9.84

- **#000000** - 21

Yes, if you have a different color background, then these values change, and you can choose for yourself, but who is going to know the hex color they want if they don't know web design? If you want to check your own contrast color, then you can do so at https://app.contrast-finder.org

When you're happy, click the top left where it says Branding to get to the top menu, and click on Homepage.

This will give you several options for your header. This is all vibes, but I personally like the magazine format because it shows both my hero post in the center and then four other recent posts.

Then, if you toggle on the "Show top posts" slider, it shows the most viewed and highest engagement posts for my publication under it. This only used to be possible if you chose the newspaper format, and I love this change.

There are no right or wrong answers here. I recommend making your hero post prominent (and pinning it to the top of your main page if you haven't done that part yet). Otherwise, it's what feels good to you.

From there, toggle on "Advanced layouts", and we can start to customize the bottom of our page. The first thing you want to do is add a Subscribe block. After that, you can make some choices that feel good to you. I have a lot of tags and sections, so I have a few different tags and sections showing. I recommend you have at least one section or tag showing because it's the only way you can have a sidebar, which is critical if you want that one-line short description to show, which we do.

So, choose at least one tag or section, and then flick on either the right or left sidebar, and put a subscribe widget right there so your one-line description can be as high on the page as possible. If you have a couple of different blocks, then add a subscribe block below them, and you're done. See, it was so easy because we did the other work already.

What about the actual writing?

Notice we didn't talk about the actual articles yet? Well, we were subtly doing that this whole time. All of this brand building, audience testing, and imagery collecting should give you a killer idea about the exact kinds of help your audience needs from you.

If you're still not sure, then you should read about a million articles from your model publications and find out the kinds of things they talk about in their most popular posts. You should be able to sort a publication by popularity, and those are the ones that resonate best for their audience.

It's probably going to give you a broad spectrum, but there will also be types of articles each publication writes. *How long are they? Are there any gaps? How could you add your unique spin to it?*

There are about a billion articles on how to write a great Substack, but I still thought that my audience needed my unique spin on it. I've also never seen an article that goes into so much depth about the methodology behind branding a publication from the ground up. I also have ways of embedding a love of marketing into all of my articles (*I hope*) that resonates with my audience.

So, while I love all the articles I read, this is my unique take on how to do it, and it's filled with things I thought were overlooked in previous articles, along with things my audience struggles with inside their own publications.

My job is to find a little pocket of the market that helps grow the community. Everything I post about goes back to that brand document and lookbook as I ask myself what to write and when to talk about it.

Metrics

What about metrics? Should you be staring at your dashboard a hundred times a day? When are metrics good, and when are they bad?

1. Metrics are good when they give you a baseline of what to expect in every post and can show you when you have a post that exceeds or underperforms those expectations.
2. Metrics are bad when you take those expectations, and they hamper you from doing something you really want to do with your publication.

For instance, sometimes, I'll have a post that performs way worse than others, even though I'm sending them all to the same audience. When that happens, I'll change the headline and the imagery to see if that helps, but sometimes you just can't blame whisks for everything wrong with humanity and get people to care...even if it's a killer post.

That said, I still think the relationship between writers and technology is an important concept to talk about, and I would have still done it even if it didn't get any traction because it reinforces the concept of my whole publication.

Tim Ferris says that he hopes that over the course of four podcast episodes, he can please 100% of his audience, but he really only cares about servicing 25% of them with any given episode.

I think that's a really good metric to think about in your own writing. ***Will 25% of the people on my list absolutely adore this post?*** Then, it's probably worth doing, even if you think it would be better to please them all. Hyperfocusing your message to resonate deeply with a small subsection of people is how you cultivate superfans.

Making these decisions is a big part of finding your voice. If you only talk about things with mass appeal, then you'll likely start sounding like every other publication. When you focus on finding what makes your view unique, then that is when you can begin separating yourself.

Weirdly, it's usually those niche articles that get the most paid members, which is the goal, right? *(Or one of the goals, at least)* It's probably because people have never seen an article like it before, and if they think only you can deliver for them, they will see the value of joining.

Homogeneity is the death of small publications. It's in embracing their unique voice that writers thrive and find an audience. Airbnb popularized the idea that the only way to scale is to do the unscaleable, and sometimes that includes writing posts that absolutely can't find traction in the mass audience because they speak to very specific people who need to hear it.

Frankly, I think almost all metrics are dumb. Worrying about engagement is dumb. Staring at a KPI dashboard is dumb.

Most of the metrics I've tracked over my career have made my business worse, not better.

There are only three metrics that I care about these days.

- Monthly subscriber growth
- # of opens
- $$$ in bank account

Some of my most beloved articles have almost no engagement. Most of my best-converting emails have no engagement. Most of my best subscribers are lurkers who just read religiously and never comment.

I'm the same way. I will share your work in my weekly roundups easier than I will like your post, even though it takes me infinitely more time.

I've never talked to many of the people who gave me the most money, and most of our best evangelists speak about my work without letting me know.

Maybe you care a lot about metrics, and that's fine, especially if you're a desert, but for the most part, I think metrics are stupid.

That's not to say I don't care at all, but the three I mentioned are the only ones that have truly moved my business forward in any real way.

No matter what, if you track more than 3-5 metrics at any one time, it will be hard to have success moving any of them in a positive direction.

Even then, you'll drive yourself crazy looking at them.

***

With Sparkle—to train myself out of looking at paid subscriber numbers on the dashboard, I focused on my 30-day views and looked at ways to reshare my work after the original share. I started with a goal of 'consistent monthly 25k views'. Now, six months on, I'm at 56k monthly views. Eyes on my work makes me happy, as does money in my bank. I'm in the UK; it's far better for me to see my business as a whole and, like Russell, check my bank account than it is to look at GAR in USD on the dashboard.

***

Pivoting

It is almost guaranteed that you will get some of this wrong, maybe all of it wrong, and have to pivot to something else. There is a lot of chatter on Substack about how to pivot well, and I happen to have written about that in *This is a NOT Book*.

People often tell me that I pivot to new lines of business very well and ask me how I do it.

I figured I would write down what I've learned about pivoting over the years. I think it comes down to a few factors.

Getting punched

There is no substitute for experience. If you don't want to get punched in the mouth yourself, then at least hire a coach who can see all the red flags coming and steer you away from them.

I can't tell you how many months of my life would have been saved by having somebody who had already been there to tell me something was a bad idea.

Of course, I'm stubborn, so I don't know if I would have listened, but I regret not having that when I was younger. I did have a good group of friends who were on the same journey as me to bounce ideas off of, though, which was helpful.

It used to take me a lot longer to pivot, though, because I didn't have the experience to see what was coming.

***

With Sparkle—I can't agree more. I invest £1000s into working with coaches, mentors, and experts every year, and this work is worth every penny. Sometimes, just one thing framed up in a new way gives you a business and/ or confidence boost to set you on a brand-new trajectory.

***

Plan

Two examples here. With Wannabe Press, we were planning to be more reliant on online sales in 2017, but that plan took three years to implement. It took hundreds, maybe thousands of hours of planning to position ourselves to make that happen.

We began implementing our plan in 2020, a couple of months before the pandemic. We were prepared to weather it when it came. Even then, it nearly tore us apart, but we were more ready than almost anyone around us.

Second, Monica and I had already run a campaign for our Kickstarter book and had a beta cohort of our Accelerator that allowed us to test all our theories before launching our program. There was some success, and we were ready to move forward eventually, so when we saw the Brandon Sanderson campaign, it allowed us to leap on it.

From there, we've spent the last couple of months building the infrastructure around it. Now, we're working on cornering the market, but it would never have happened if we hadn't prepared long in advance to make that pivot when the opportunity presented itself.

In both cases, we had a long-term plan that could be shortened or lengthened depending on a host of factors. Planning 2-5 steps ahead and having contingency plans in case things went wrong or right was essential for our pivot.

Develop skills

I've been a one-man show for most of my adult life, and because of that, I've learned a lot about how to run a business. I'm an expert at book publishing and Kickstarter, but I also have a degree in journalism, which allowed me to master virtual conferences, podcasts, and about a hundred other things, from accounting to contract negotiation.

All of that allowed me to pivot all over the place because I dug deep into every aspect of business and learned how it worked to build a solid foundation under myself.

I sold courses for years before the Accelerator blew up, appeared at hundreds of conventions, and both guested on and hosted tons of podcasts before partnering with Monica.

There is a curiosity needed to pivot well, specifically for exploring things that might be helpful in the future, even if it's not helpful now.

The main reason I can pivot well is that I explored every avenue. Even though I abandoned most of them, when they became relevant again, I brushed off those skills and could move on them almost immediately.

Trust

Even though I know a lot about a lot of things, the thing I know most is what needs to be offloaded so I can focus on my own zone of genius.

I do not do my own taxes, edit my own books, do my own covers, proofread my own stuff, edit my own podcast, or...well, you get the point. Monica is even better at this than I am, and she's taught me a lot about offloading things to other people.

While I know how to do those things, I know what I don't want to do and what I don't do well enough to matter.

Knowing the landscape allows me to speak intelligently about many subjects and then offload the work to contractors, giving them a good sense of what needs to get done so it gets done right the first time.

***

With Sparkle—I have VAs who support me with growth, podcast edits, and admin. They are worth their weight in gold. I have a list of Substack adjacent support on my home page navigation —everything from Substack-focused VAS to PR, coaches to designers. Check it out—it's called Substack S.O.S.

***

Don’t be precious

Most things service you until they don't, and when they stop servicing me, I jettison them quickly.

Moreover, I notice when things are not serving me well in advance, and that allows me to abandon them before they crash-land at my feet.

Whether it was my Complete Creative podcast, running author marketing for clients, or ending series before the bottom dropped out, I have always been able to tell the warning signs (making less money/having few listens with each installment, fewer social media engagements, etc.), and pivot away from them.

I've also been able to integrate new things that serviced me into my arsenal seamlessly because I planned for a long time before I pulled the trigger on anything, making sure it fit with my audience.

I'm usually a year or so ahead of my slate, so I can move my marketing in whatever way I need to make things seem natural.

Most people are weighed down, especially after years of doing this work, with the past, especially things that don't work or barely break even. They keep writing that series that barely breaks even or keep servicing that client who is more trouble than they are worth.

I have found that being able to disassociate the work from marketing has helped me incredibly to pivot to new things.

This also means that you should liberally cut things you are developing which don't work for you. At the beginning of the pandemic, I was developing a membership called Happy Pivot about pivoting. After developing it for months, I realized it was too far out of my lane and abandoned it.

I spent a lot of time on it, and most people would probably have kept going, but I do not believe in the sunk cost fallacy. If something won't serve me in the long term, then no matter when I figure that out, it needs to be cut and abandoned or integrated into something that will work in the long term.

Notice, though, long term doesn't mean forever. I hesitate even to say long term because something could service me for one launch, and if it scratches an itch in me, then it's worth doing, as long as I'm ready to cut ties with it shortly after and people who buy it have a good experience with the product. I have a whole suite of books and courses I only launched once that did just that, but they are not the kind of thing I build my business on or count on past that one singular launch.

Pivot

Yes, some things need time to finish, like a long series, but that doesn't mean you can't pivot in other areas of your life/business.

You can keep one thing dragging along with one hand while pivoting with the other.

This year, I'm spending my time mostly shuttering three series (Godsverse Chronicles, Ichabod Jones: Monster Hunter, and Cthulhu is Hard to Spell). However, at the same time, Monica and I spun up a whole new business, launched a podcast, and are in the middle of a second Kickstarter launch for our series.

This is mostly possible because those series were complete in 2021, so I could focus on launching them instead of writing them, but you don't have to pivot with your whole life. You can keep certain things going, spin down other things, and spin up still more, allowing you to keep pivoting.

Because that's the biggest thing I've learned—there is ALWAYS a pivot. The reason people aren't very good at it is that they are waiting for the one perfect pivot, but it's usually, almost always, a series of little pivots that slide in and out of your life.

The better you can get at constantly being in flux, the less anything can knock you down because you'll be ready to pivot and allow it to flow through you.

Finally, this life is long, and you can always learn how to pivot better, even if you're not great at it now.

The good and bad is that in a couple of months, most people won't remember your old brand, and those that do won't care if you keep giving them that good value. That said, you should plan to stick with one name for as long as possible, which is why all this exhausting work is worth it.

I'm actually less concerned with your failure than I am about your success. The minute a writer has success, they immediately start to double down and quadruple down on what's working until they burn out.

I have watched this play out over and over again. People keep filling their plates until they burn out because they think if they aren't working every minute of every day, then they come across as ungrateful for the opportunity. Then, that will lead to everyone hating them and ultimately falling back to obscurity and failure.

However, they will fail again. Every one of us will mostly fail.

In my experience, life is a series of occasional successes filled in by slowly escalating failures until the next success.

The biggest predictor of success isn't how big a splash you make; it's how long you can survive, and you won't survive long going harder than your body can handle.

There is a time for doubling down, but it's when you are well-leveraged to take advantage of an opportunity without killing yourself to make it happen...and you won't be able to do that if you are already overleveraged.

If you are too busy to do the things you like and can never get ahead, you are overleveraged and in time debt. To get out of that debt, you need to find leverage points in your business to exploit.

I am not a particularly hard worker. I am just very good at finding leverage points and knocking over dominos. People are often surprised when I tell them how little I actually work because I generally seem so busy. But that is because I am excellent at leveraging myself and creating space to say yes to great opportunities and turning down bad ones.

It is possible to make the same money in 4 hours a day as you can in 16, and it is possible to create massive revenue in a very short amount of time. You just have to leverage yourself properly. It breaks my heart to see how so many people I know work without getting any gain.

How do you find those opportunities? By slowing down long enough to analyze your previous successes and plan for the next one strategically. When you're burning the candle at both ends, you can't do the kind of thinking that will actually help you level up.

Since you'll probably fail anyway, and you're definitely going to fail more than you succeed, you should probably learn to revel in the failures and position yourself to make the next success bigger than the last one.

I think the beauty of marketing is in the fuzzy bits. One of the biggest misconceptions about marketing is that it will give you the perfect way to do everything, but in my experience, it's not about that at all. It's all about the fuzzy bits between the gutters, like comics.

Marketing is asking yourself how the right people who need your message the most can find you the quickest and know they are in the right place.

If the right people find your publication and don't know it's for them, they will leave and never hear it. I am sure that's not what you want.

If the wrong people find your publication and think it is for them, you will have a bad time because your email will be full of people you don't seek to serve.

When you get the branding right, and the right people can find your message more quickly, that is when you have harmony and live in your bliss.

It's also when it starts to make sense to invest money in finding new people.

Notes on Substack Notes

On Notes, you can:

- Tag another writer using the @ symbol and their writer handle.
- Restack a post or quote from a post (yours or others).
- Crowdsource information.
- Write a stand-alone note.
- Share a photo or video.
- You have some editing and formatting tools there, too.
- You can mute or block other users.

Notes is Substack's inbuilt social media feed

In my (Claire's) opinion, it's a bit like Twitter but kinder, more sophisticated and less aggressive. It's a BRILLIANT place to build connections and grow your following and your subscribers.

You can post a short note or a longer note, and folks can 'comment underneath'. It can be seen by everyone on the Substack network, but in reality, it's probably only going to be your subs/followers who are online and perhaps some of theirs, too. If you get a wild or spammy comment underneath, you can delete it.

There are no ads, but writers/creators do advertise their work/writing/book projects. It's chronological, and Notes can stick around for up to five days, sometimes longer.

Notes are shown to your followers and your subscribers who are there and scrolling. Likes and replies boost the Note to stay around for longer. Substack sometimes shares Notes in their round-ups, too. We should ALWAYS be supportive of our colleagues. It's hard enough to advertise; throw a heart in.

You can grab the URL of a Note and pop it into one of your posts, and it will automatically embed.

Why Notes?

Notes launched in April 2023, five years after Substack was born and is still being shaped by us, the creatives and writers (who also read) who use it for connection, building kinship and finding like-minded colleagues AND subscribers.

Notes help bring folks to your publication to subscribe, and they may also follow you instead.

You can write a Note about anything you like. You can share writing, yours or someone else's.

You can share photos or snippets of video, and you can share links, you can quote people.

You can invite people to conversations, crowdsource info, test ideas...

It's a 24/7 party, and EVERYONE's invited.

Types of Notes

- A Quote.
- A restack (from your or someone else's post).
- An update.

This chapter compiles some of the BEST posts and advice I've seen on using Notes, plus my own take from the early days. I have free video tutorials on this topic, too.

A note on going viral...

As research for this chapter, between March and May 2024, I put out Notes that I expect to do well. Inspiring quotes, sophisticated writer cheerleading, crowdfunding asks...

The one that took off the most? Photos of our new puppy at 3 weeks old with her brothers and sisters!

I also took a week off posting Notes to check the impact on my monthly subscriber numbers (down around 80). There will be other factors at play, but in reality, I know there are a huge number of new eyes on my work because of Notes and my interaction there.

During my research period, there were two examples of writers going viral on Notes (over 1000 likes). Unfortunately, one of the writers took their notes down as the influx was too much to manage.

One was someone who had over 1000 subs arrive in 12 hours, and with that, some jarring connections/spam. One I don't know; I never got to talk to him...he left Substack.

My take is we would have to think through how to feel ready for the entire internet to land on our doorstep if we tried to make a Note go viral, and honestly, I don't know if you want to aim for that.

It is better to build relationships and share what you want to share. I usually do a couple of Notes every day and join in with conversations, but 2-3 a week would be enough to grow your publication.

Intention is everything...

Here's Substack's first-ever post about Notes...

"We started Substack in 2017 because we wanted the internet to be better for writers and readers. We were dismayed with the clickbait and content farms, the listicles and liars, the cheap outrage and culture wars. We thought there could be something better if writers and readers were given more control and treated as a higher priority than advertisers, and if culture makers could find financial dignity without needing to sublimate themselves to attention games and corporate marketing budgets. "We believe that what you read matters," we said, and we meant it.

So we set about building a system that fosters deep connections and quality over shallow engagement and dopamine hacks. We turned away from advertising and the attention economy and toward subscriptions and direct relationships. We believed that something beautiful could emerge from marrying the internet's powers with a business model that puts writers and readers in charge, that rewards great work with money, and that protects the free press and free speech. We came to believe that this model—a subscription network—could form the basis of a new economic engine for culture."

Notes—part of your creative workflow?

I asked Kristi Keller, who writes Unstack Substack and who is a brilliant mind on Notes, to share with us:

"When I receive emails from fellow Substackers asking for growth tips, I only ever have one tip. That tip is called NOTES, and aside from writing great content, if you learn to use Notes properly, it's all you need to grow organically. I use ZERO social media outside of Substack. So, how does one use Notes properly? Stop promoting your links and start being relatable.

I know that sounds counterintuitive because we all want to drive eyeballs to our story links, but that's not how engagement seems to work on Substack.

Every single day, we're inundated with links begging, "Please go read my stuff!" But nobody needs more stuff. We need more feelings of community. We want to relate to each other, and there's no better way to do it than to post a note that is easily digestible and highly relatable.

I've had several notes go viral with 1K - 2K likes, but there was the one in particular that attracted over 6000+ likes and 500+ restacks. It was a simple inspirational quote.

And it earned me over 700 subscribers within a 30-day period.

People are exhausted from being advertised to and linked to death. Facebook and Instagram have that market wrapped up. Substack is a much more intimate community.

The next time you're looking for a growth hack, try putting yourself out there rather than just another link."

We love this wisdom from Kristi and would highly recommend that you subscribe to her publication.

You can use Notes on your desktop or in the app. There's really no reason not to jump in unless you are avoiding all social media-based experiences.

You have the power to curate your feed, so make it a nice place to be. Think about being inspired and educated. Mute or block anything that isn't that.

In June 2024, I mentored a Sparkle on Substack client with a strategy for her first Note. It went viral. It was the perfect blend of cuteness and talent. At the time of writing, it's sitting at almost 14,000 likes, over 900 comments, and 281 restacks. It's driven 4000 subscribers, some pledges, and a ton of sales. My client is a professional illustrator. She shared an illustration of a dog that had also done well on her Instagram at a time of her choosing that often works for her on socials. I gave her two tips.

One—people on Notes like pets and always dogs. Two—tell them how you're feeling about arriving on Substack. The rest is down to the Note capturing a lot of imagination in a short space of time.

First up "following/followers...

As we've learned on many a social media platform over the years...

You will see when you subscribe to a publication that Substack automatically checks the follow and subscribe boxes for you. They then ask you if you want to uncheck those boxes.

It could be (like me) that you uncheck them all...but given the influx of followers some of us have had, it could be that folks aren't unchecking the subscribe/follow box...

When you follow someone, you follow their Notes on Substack. You do not receive their emails/publication update posts.

You can check their Notes 'feed' and see what they've posted by heading to the writer profile.

Categories, daily leaderboards on Notes

Substack has lots of categories, and sometimes you'll see the top 5 performing pots for that category. You can toggle your interests on and off so you only see the topics you're interested in. Posts chosen for these daily leaderboards tend to have a lot of engagement (likes, comments, shares).

Notes that do well and things to consider when composing a Note...

(Not an exhaustive list)

There's a secret algorithm on Notes. Here are the things it likes:

- Pets—cats/dogs but really any pets.
- GREAT writing.
- Talking about Substack.
- Talking about writing.
- Talking about books/book deals.
- Joyful things.
- Funny things.
- Writer solidarity.
- Moments of magic.
- Moments of the mundane that feel like magic.
- Controversy (sometimes).
- Long Notes.
- Short Notes.
- Easy to engage with Notes.
- Easy-to-like (heart) notes.
- Writing/memes/posts that build community...
- Messy photos.

- Beautiful photos.
- Cheerleading words.
- Words that invite a reaction.
- Things that stop the scroll.
- When you (@) tag a writer like this.
- "Things that did well on Facebook in 2012" – Russell Nohelty.

It could also be that team Substack has a big orange button in their office.

A button they like to press while making a cuppa to boost Notes and get them seen more—who knows (?). One thing I do know is it's a ton of fun to be at the Notes party!

Reading and recommendations

Russell and I massively advocate for taking up reading like it's an Olympic sport on Substack. This is especially important in the first six months, but you might also find a balance to incorporate reading slots into your weeks. I read in the evenings every single evening—I barely miss a post from those I subscribe to—it's a total pleasure to be connected.

That's to say we want you to READ a lot of Substacks. There's a balance here. We don't want to read so much that we think our work is pants in comparison, or we take on a new tone of voice. It keeps you reading across the categories you are interested in. Like the posts, leave comments, start conversations—be a supportive colleague.

Utilizing Recommendations to grow your Substack

Over 4000 of my subscribers have come from recommendations from other Substack writers in the last two years. Over 350 from just two writers.

Recommendations is a magical Substack back-office portal where surprises and treats are a-plenty! Look for the tab in your writer dashboard. At the top, it will tell you how many subscribers have come through Recommendations and how many publications are recommending you. There is also a breakdown listing individual publications that have recommended you and how many folks have come across to subscribe. Your top five are usually great people to collaborate with.

As you scroll down, you'll see how many subscribers your recommendations have sent others. They have the same data—you're already colleagues and friends! Where do you want to take the relationship?

If you click Manage, you will find the space to write 'blurbs'—press the three dots, and you can type in some kind words. A writer may share these publicly or add them to their welcome page.

The right recommendation can change the business of your Substack overnight, especially if a creator is importing audiences.

Social proof

There's something about the words of others that adds that something extra! It's reassuring and helpful, and it can be a key part of subscriber decision-making.

It's also very reassuring to read the words people choose to use to describe your work—they are often different from the words you use. One of the first kind quotes I received still lives at the top of my About page with the writer linked. It reads:

"Claire is the Queen of Substack"

I remember receiving it and thinking WOW, that is high praise indeed! I felt honored and shy all at the same time. A few days later, after talking to my husband, I claimed the title and popped it on my About page. It's not that I think I am the 'only queen' of Substack these days, but often people find me, and they don't know of other Substack educators, so it is the reassurance they need that I know my stuff!

There are lots of ways to grow and add 'social proof' to your Substack.

Breathing in gratitude for the kind words people share is one of the nicest parts of being a Substack creator.

One of the things I do once a month as a creative practice is check in on the following five ways people leave me feedback:

- Recommendations here on Substack.
- Transformational Case Studies.
- Testimonials.
- Kind Words (screenshots from posts/Notes etc.).
- Surveys.

Try it. Testimonial Tuesday!

Our brains like patterns and creative practices we can embed.

Every Tuesday, you open a document or a Substack draft, and you pour in any screen grabs, kind words or other notes of support you've received. Even if you forget to do it one week, you will still have tens of opportunities every single year to see how appreciated your work is. You'll also have a ton of words of social proof to pepper through your About page, to use in posts, on your website, or other socials if relevant.

Try it. Kickstart your month with Reciprocity and write Recommendations

At the start of the month, I pop into the Recommendations tab, and I write 3-5 blurbs for other Substack publications I've been enjoying—I do this every single month. While I'm there, I see what I might have missed in the way of others who recommend my publications, and I recommend them back if I've enjoyed their work.

When you subscribe to a new publication, you'll be offered some others to subscribe to. There's an algorithm at play here, and I know it works for me.

When you pay to subscribe to a publication, make sure you leave a 'paid subscriber note'. Not only will you make someone's day, but the writer might also share it and tag you. Your publication name will appear on the graphic they download if you give permission.

5 ideas to grow social proof for your Substack Publication and to reassure you on hard days...

- Recommendations—once a month, at the start of the month, write some recommendations for some other Substacks you've enjoyed, and tag them in Notes if you want to. Shoot for three and see if you can write more than that.

- Case Studies—good for memberships. If relevant, once a season—share a case study—this is NOT the same as a screenshot testimonial. A case study should talk about where the client/ student was before your offer, their journey with your offer/ work, and what their life is like now. Important details to include are the length of time to see results, the main pain points before joining your offer, and how your offer/publication specifically helped them. Aim for four paragraphs.

- Testimonials—these can pop up anytime, but you can also ask for them. I do this once per year and give a framework to help folks express how I've helped them and how my work and words have impacted them.

- Kind Words (screenshots)—sometimes folks say lovely things about our work and toward us in posts or notes, grab screenshots and put them in a folder as and when you get tagged in them. You can extract the words later or use them as they are and insert them into 'sales' posts.

- Surveys—design your own survey in Substack or use the poll feature here to invite your readers to engage. Click 'more' at the top right of your composer, and you'll find the polls there. Polls work super well, and surveys can also give you a more intimate insight into how your readers/paid subs/members feel.

What is invested shall return...

Are you wondering how you might start to receive these magical messages in your inboxes?

Leave some for others—leave long and considered paid subscriber notes if you upgrade, long and considered blurbs in recommendations once a month—make someone's day!

Tag folks in Notes, restack, and be supportive and social if it feels right. Educate your community on how to leave recommendations, and they'll soon be popping in to recommend your work.

Maximizing Substack for each Author Ecosystem

Most authors I (Russell) talk with ask some form of the question, "How did you succeed on Substack?" Of course, what they really mean is, "How can I succeed at Substack?"

While I can't give you personalized advice, and you are a living, breathing human reading this asynchronously, the next best thing is to show you how each ecosystem can best utilize Substack to grow their author career.

I have spent hundreds of hours on Substack trying to learn everything I could about the platform. Meanwhile, we've talked to hundreds of authors about their ecosystems. Together, we've molded those two conversations to create an overview of how I think each ecosystem can utilize Substack.

One thing I will say is that if you're looking for fiction, there are roughly 300 fiction publications that write fiction. I have a ton of fiction available in my publication, but there is not the same amount of fiction as there is in nonfiction. Luckily, the fiction community here is hugely supportive, and they are great at supporting each other.

However, if you are specifically looking for a deep well of fiction readers/ authors to mine immediately, you will likely be disappointed. If you're looking for a supportive, growing community, then you're in the right place. Fiction is in its infancy here, but I think it will grow into something magical with time and support.

Let's talk about how each Author Ecosystem can use Substack to grow success. If you want to learn all about Monica and my Author Ecosystems archetype system, you can find much more information at: https://authorecosystems.substack.com

Desert

Advantages: The secret power of a Desert is optimization. Deserts can look at a newsfeed and understand the underlying code powering it. If you've ever seen people talk about "gaming the system", that's probably a Desert. They love finding ways to "win the conversation".

When you start looking at Notes, the first thing a Desert will realize is that the algorithm powering Substack is very basic. It's not quite Facebook circa 2004, but it absolutely reminds me of 2010-2012 Facebook, and a lot of the strategies that no longer work on other platforms still work here.

For instance, while the feed is not chronological, every time your post is commented on, you'll be boosted to the top of people's feeds. Additionally, commenting on other people's posts helps you be seen by more people as well because the last comment is shown to people scrolling. If you can make charming and well-thought-out comments, you will start to see your subscriber count going up.

Challenges: Growth on Substack is slow. Deserts often tire of platforms where they can't see exponential growth quickly, and Substack is a very small platform compared to TikTok, Amazon, Facebook, Instagram, etc. The strength of a Desert is being able to plug into the "winning" conversation and ride those gains to success fast. Then, they find a new trend and ride that, building momentum by finding that wave consistently.

There is absolutely a prevailing narrative on Substack, but while a bigger platform will have a dozen or more conversations happening at one time between millions of people, Substack usually has 1-2 between thousands, so you'll have to plant more in a couple of categories to have fast growth.

Additionally, Substack rewards subject expertise. Deserts are incredible at writing on any subject as long as it's popular. They take joy in the writing work as much as, or more than, the topic. While Substack certainly has "general" Substack publications that deal with a lot of topics, they generally have a theme or tone that unites them. For a Desert who's used to donning a hundred personalities depending on the job, it can feel limiting.

Grassland

Advantages: Substack is tailor-made for Grasslands, who are built for depth. Substack rewards subject expertise and extensive knowledge of a topic, which is exactly how Grasslands "win" the marketing game. Readers are more than happy to geek out on a topic with you all day, every day for years.

Additionally, Substack rewards "putting pennies in the bank" by slowly building your platform over time. There are multiple articles about people's success on Substack that started with somebody investing in their publication for years and slowly building over time until they started to see exponential growth almost overnight.

While this might seem like a nightmare scenario for other ecosystems, it's often how Grasslands prefer to exist. They have no problem talking about a trend they spot for years before they reap the rewards when people finally catch up to them.

Additionally, one of the best growth strategies on Substack is to incorporate ongoing conversations into articles while keeping them on-topic, which is something Grasslands have the preternatural ability to do naturally.

Challenges: Substack is great for depth, but there is also an ongoing conversation happening through Notes. The biggest challenge for Grasslands is the inability or unwillingness to join that ongoing conversation. Most Grasslands came to Substack to write long and nerd out about their topic, but they miss plugging into the conversation to help improve the timeliness of their writing.

Many Grasslands are so busy going deep on a topic that they miss the ability to influence that ongoing conversation. While the conversation on Notes might not always be about your topic, that's no reason to avoid trying to influence it. I pick up subscribers every day by communicating with them on Notes. Plus, often, the posts I make on Notes become the seeds of future articles.

I do work in the author growth space, though, so often by simply existing in this space, I can find new subscribers, but that only worked because I embraced my inner Grassland and found a topic with a lot of depth that I thought would be of interest to the Substack audience for a long time.

Don't forget that any social media platform is best utilized by finding the intersectionality between your interests and how the conversation works on the platform already. If you can plug into that conversation by harnessing your inner Desert, then your natural strengths as a Grassland will help you carry the day.

Tundra

Advantages: Tundras can harness excitement and stack tropes on top of each other like no other ecosystem, and that works well on Substack. The conversation on Substack is often cyclical, so if you can harness your inner Grassland and write evergreen articles about those topics, you will be able to bring people into your ecosystem while their excitement is at its highest.

You must be careful not to sound like a broken record pitching the same thing over and over, but as long as you infuse everything with excitement, you should be able to keep your content fresh.

Tundras love figuring out how to position their work in the market. Therefore, it was easy to distinguish myself from other publications by the sheer length and depth of my articles (*they tend to be 5,000+ words*). I try to stack 2-3 popular evergreen tropes into each article so that as many people can get value from a single piece of content as possible.

My promotion strategy looks a lot like a mini version of the rolling waves I usually talk about, which are ideal for a Tundra. Every article is released on a Wednesday, and I then crescendo my marketing. I have also found a lot of value in creating a weekly roundup with dozens of other articles I loved to help harness other people's excitement to help drive marketing for my own articles.

Challenges: Subscriptions never end...like ever. Tundras are used to building excitement for something and then moving on to the next thing, but with Substack, they must constantly keep going. There is always another article due to satisfy the readers, and it's a big shock to the system.

As such, I've had to learn to conserve my energy more because Substack is a marathon, not a sprint. Instead of building up huge excitement for every launch, I've had to find more sustainable ways of doing less while maintaining the same cadence of my ideal launch cycle.

Additionally, Tundras must remember to reference their vault of information as they continue through their Substack journey. We live to launch and move on, but Substack is about referencing and re-referencing your work forever. I found that using sections to help build a big vault of content helps keep continued momentum without constantly needing to build that excitement every day of my life.

Mostly, you really do have to harness your inner Grassland and become much better at "putting pennies in the bank" to maximize your success with Substack. Likely, you will also get a lot of value from doing PBS-style pledge drives a few times a year to focus attention on Substack and harness that excitement, which would be a launch strategy uniquely suited to Tundras.

Forest

Advantages: Substack is all about community, and Forests thrive in those settings. Since Substack is essentially a membership community, Forests should feel right at home with things like Recommendations and using sections to increase value to paid members.

Additionally, the Substack community is very interested in reading publications with unique voices, which is where Forests shine. The more unique you can make your articles, the better chance you have for success. This is a huge boon for Forests, who win at marketing by embracing their inner weirdo.

Forests are also very concerned with improving the human experience for others, which fits in very well with the ethos of Notes. The more "love" you can spread to connect with people on an individual level, the more success you will have, and that's one of a Forest's biggest strengths.

Challenges: Forests have a hard time writing anything that is not 100% aligned with their inner north star. They are the opposite of Deserts in that respect, but part of succeeding on Substack is being part of the ongoing narrative on the platform.

The more you can merge your north star with what's happening in the overall conversation happening on the platform, the quicker you will have success.

Forests have a hard time building momentum anywhere because their interests are wide-ranging and disparate. Still, if you can do the branding work early and somehow find a way to connect everything, even in a tenuous way, you'll have more success.

Communities are all about in-jokes and mutually agreed-on norms, but it's important to remember while those things are incredible when you're "in on the joke", they can be intimidating to outsiders. Forests have problems when they fail to look outside their group and be inviting to others, so make sure to be as welcoming to those outside of your community as those inside of it.

One of the major reasons to be on Substack is for the organic growth you get through their recommendation engine and network effects. Make sure to use them effectively to scale. Otherwise, you might find more success on Patreon, which was designed to shower love on people already in on the joke.

Aquatic

Advantages: Aquatics want to do all the things all the time, and Substack has lots of formats to play with, including their own podcasting system. They allow you to set up sections to silo off different projects from each other and play with transmedia across audio, video, photography, art, comics, and text.

There are tons of different subcommunities on Substack that you can use to build your publication. You can create a photography project for #photostack, a film for #filmstack, a comic for #comicstack, a choose-your-own-adventure for #gamestack, and keep creating new ways to bring people into your universe. None of these niches are particularly huge, but together, they can add up to a powerful audience.

You can also use the hunger for new content in these smaller audiences to help build excitement for your projects with a lot of organic reach. Then, when they're inside your universe, they will find how many other amazing formats and projects they can sink their teeth into to fall deeper in love with your brand.

Challenges: Substack only allows one price point for subscriptions, but Aquatics generally have multiple formats that require different price points, so it will be hard to find one price point to service their whole audience. One thing they can think about is using their Founding member tier for their more resource-intensive formats. Or they can price their whole publication at a higher level (*$20+*) than would be normal with other ecosystems (*$5-$10/mo is the norm*).

Additionally, while there ***are*** different niches within Substack, Aquatics might not be able to enter into the main conversation often enough to scale fast. With a platform like Reddit or Facebook, even the small niches are huge, but with Substack, there are generally only 1-2 main conversations happening at the same time.

Hopefully, you already have a ton of different formats to play with before entering the Substack ecosystem because it would take a ton of paid members to scale beyond the written word without also utilizing something like Kickstarter or Patreon to fill out your ecosystem. However, if you want to find a place to create one monster audience from a bunch of formats, then Substack could work great for you.

Final thoughts on ecosystems on Substack...

Substack can work for any ecosystem, but it works even better if you can harness a little bit of every ecosystem. If you can mine the conversations to stay on top of the reader's mind like a Desert while also harnessing your inner Grassland to go deep on a niche, you will have a powerful combination for success. If you can additionally stack evergreen topics and harness excitement like a Tundra while building a community like a Forest and expanding out to different formats like an Aquatic, you'll do even better. ***It's a bit like Voltron.*** Those kitties are powerful alone, but together, they are unstoppable.

Newsletter growth stages

I (Russell) was talking with a newsletter operator a little while ago and got to talking about newsletter stages and places where writers get stuck in their growth journey. While I understand that not everyone even cares about growth, I think it's important to understand data even if you make different choices.

To help aid this discussion, it's important to bring in Writer MBA's Author Ecosystems framework again as we talk about the levels of newsletter growth to inform our conversation.

Here are the five levels Monica and I found through our research. Please remember, these ecosystems are about marketing and sales success, so ***if you are not even ready to think about that kind of thing, then you would be a Level 0.***

- **Level 1**—*Inert.* Authors at this level don't even know how to start doing things because it's so overwhelming. They are pulled in every direction and feel like they are drowning in information from every direction. To get out of this level, you need to start doing something, and it doesn't matter much what you do.

- **Level 2**—*Developing.* Authors at this level have started doing things, which is great, but nothing is working. They follow all the best practices as best they can but are failing at everything they try. If you want to get to the next level, you have to find something that works and latch onto it. ***NOTE:*** *You probably won't know your* *ecosystem until you get out of this stage, and that's okay. Until you know what works, you are just using what feels right to you. Once you know what works, then you'll have a better handle on it.*

- **Level 3**—*Emergent.* Authors at this level have found something that works, but they are also doing all sorts of other things that aren't working. To get out of this level, you need to shed everything that's not working and double down on things that are working for your ecosystem.

- **Level 4**—*Evolved.* Authors at this level have fully embraced their ecosystem and are making money, but they are capped out at what they can earn without evolving beyond what they've been doing. To exit this level, you need to integrate other ecosystems into your author business.

- **Level 5**—*Expanded.* At this top level, authors have found ways to integrate new bits into their business that help them continuously grow.

These don't map perfectly to the phases below, but they should give you some context for where you should be on your journey as you grow your audience and network.

I also want to point out that your ***network*** and your ***fandom/audience*** are two different things.

Your ***network*** consists of the other creators, publishers, and operators with whom you promote your work, write guest posts for, and whose audiences you borrow to build your audience. Your ***fandom/audience*** is the readers who love your work. Sometimes, there will be overlap, but they are distinct.

Each of the phases below represents bottlenecks I have seen writers hit their heads against, and hopefully, this will give you some context of how to break through those blocks.

Breaking through barriers

When people ask the hardest thing about growing an author business, it's that it's relatively easy to get to the top 20% of writers in the world but impossible to get into the top 5%. Most of getting into the top 50% is about craft, and then, with some cheap tricks, you can blow past most other writers who refuse to do even the minimum amount of promotion.

However, it gets harder and harder the further you move up until, at some point, you get stuck because the power law curve starts working in earnest.

If you are the 10th-best (or 100th-best, depending on the size) plumber in your city, you are probably making a pretty decent living. If you're the 50th-best accountant in your area, you probably have a pretty good job.

Yes, the absolute best accountants are doing better than you, probably even significantly better than you, but you can still make a decent living, even if you are in the middle of the curve.

That's not true in creative businesses, which have the most brutal power law curve of any other industry.

Authors at the top make exponentially more than the people at the bottom or even in the middle, which means that the more successful you get, the harder it is to get more successful because, at the top, people really, really care about staying at the top.

The people at the top are all household names, and you're competing with them for reader dollars. So, you need to know what you're doing.

The other thing is that all the money in publishing is held by the top 10% of the industry, so they are incentivized to know how to market their work. The closer you get to that top 10%, the harder it becomes.

Additionally, for the early part of a writer's career, they can get pretty far just by learning the craft. They can write their way out and grow their audience, but eventually, this stops working because everyone at their level is a terrific writer. There is a logarithmic curve to the gains writing can give you.

Eventually, you have to learn marketing if you want to grow, especially these days. Think about it like this: to get from 1% to 2%, you have to do very little work. However, it compounds with every percentile. So, to get to the 90th percentile, you have to expend as much effort as you did to get from the 1st to the 89th percentile.

Then, to get to the 9th percentile, you have to expend as much effort as it took to get from the 1st-90th percentile...that doubles your effort to get not very far at all. Or at least it doesn't look very far, but it's actually everything.

On top of that, it's just really hard to notice growth while it's happening. You could spend months working on a problem with no results, and then one day, it snaps forward, and it feels like you grow tenfold in a single night.

Phase 1—0-100 subscribers

At this stage, you have literally no idea what is going on, and that's okay. Monica and I would call this a Level 1 ecosystem. With Level 1 ecosystems, you're flailing, and you're not even sure what you are doing. You are probably not doing anything, or at least anything consistently. The best thing you can do here? Anything. Literally, anything, good or bad, so you can start to find purchase. ***A Level 2 ecosystem is one where the writer is doing things, even if they are all the wrong things.***

You can probably get to 100, or close to it, through your friend and family network, and that's cool. Most people's first readers are their friends and family, and yes, many of them might be there to humor you or to encourage you, but hey, it's something, right? Everyone has been there, including me.

Phase 2—100-1,000 subscribers

Once you are doing something, anything, and you have a small base of subscribers, you should start expanding your network. It's not a great idea to do this too early because, frankly, your stuff might not be very good or consistent. Once you have a reliable network and readers and hopefully some encouragement that you are doing a good job, it's time to start building your network.

There will be a time when you say, "Oh, I got to this point, and I'm not growing anymore". It might be at 20 or 100 subscribers, but once you get as far as you can on your own and your writing is good, it's time to build some relationships.

All writers have networks—the more successful the writer, the more powerful the network. Anyone who tells you differently is lying to you, themselves, or both.

You've already moved past a Level 1 ecosystem to a Level 2. You're doing things, but it's a lot of the wrong things. If you are doing the right things, then it's completely by accident. This stage is about moving through that into Level 3, where you're doing at least one right thing consistently and with intention, even if you're doing a lot of the wrong things, too.

Most of your growth in this phase is about finding other writers in your niche to network with and start sharing each other's articles with your respective audiences. Yes, you will almost certainly subscribe to each other's publications and support each other, but the goal is to take all your small audiences, cross-pollinate them, and end up with a bigger, more powerful audience because of it.

Writers often get caught in the trap of selling to other writers, but what they ***should*** be doing is promoting with other writers, creating guest posts for each other's publications, and finding ways to grow together.

A great example of this was our *Mon sters and Other Scary Shit* anthology. I invited over 50 collaborators to build an anthology with me. Though nobody had a huge network, we were able to raise $27,000+ on Kickstarter from 600+ backers, and that launched my whole career. A lot of small audiences created a big audience.

Phase 3—1,000-10,000 subscribers

Now you have some juice. You, and hopefully your network, have pretty decent audiences, and it's time to start making some money at this stage. If you're out ahead of your network, then it's time to pull them up to your level. ***Only good things happen if your network levels up together.***

People ask me all the time how many subscribers I think you need to have a thriving business. While you can make a business with far less than even 1,000, depending on your niche, in the publishing game, I think 10,000 engaged readers is a good barometer. Once I hit 10,000 subscribers, I was able to launch enough books and products a year to make a go of it without burning out my audience.

That doesn't mean you can't monetize earlier. I started monetizing with zero subscribers, but if you're looking for benchmarks, 1,000 is a good number of subscribers before you can hope to become a Substack bestseller, for instance. Even by their wildly inflated estimates, only 5-10% of your audience will convert to paid, which means you need at least 1,000 subscribers to hit 100 paid subscribers.

I also think 1,000 subscribers who engage with your work (30-60% open rate) get you used to dealing with an audience. You've probably gone through the "oh my god, everyone is unsubscribing" blues once or twice and built up some resilience to it. Mindset is so much of this game.

As you grow, people will give you less of the benefit of the doubt, so you really should be a bit seasoned before you get to this stage.

You've probably been doing this a while, too, and have a collection of good essays so that when more people come in, they will be able to see your best work. Along with going paid, I think you should consider running a Kickstarter or launch for a collection of your best essays. People are almost always going to have an easier time giving you $20 for a book than buying a recurring subscription until they are a fan of your work.

Phase 4—10,000-25,000 subscribers

You now have a pretty decent business going for yourself. You have fans, real hardcore fans of your work, and on some level, you are rocking and rolling. However, you're probably being yoked down by a bunch of stuff that's not working. If you haven't already, then this phase is all about shedding things that don't work and doubling down on the stuff that is working for you.

To get from a Level 3 to a Level 4 ecosystem, it's all about shedding what's holding you down and finding one reliable monetization path that you can come back to again and again. This means testing and testing and testing to make sure you have reliable data and robust experience.

The most important thing you figure out in this phase is what you can lean on when all the chips are down.

For years, my thing was conventions. Whenever I needed money, I went to a new convention and made up for my budget shortfall. With the pandemic that became Kickstarter, and it's still Kickstarter to this day. When all the chips are down, I know I can launch a campaign and reliably raise some money there.

Additionally, you're probably going to have to start advertising here, if not before. Yes, you might go viral or have some huge social media platform that delivers, but you generally can't even touch 10,000 subscribers without advertising on some significant level.

I know audience growth isn't everyone's cup of tea, but if you want to learn how to make a sustainable business that can support your weird proclivities, it's about building a robust audience that will buy from you. The bigger that audience becomes, the weirder you can get with it.

Phase 5—25,000-50,000 subscribers

I was not going to break down these upper-tier phases because so few people are interested in expanding beyond 25,000 subscribers. Still, there are some things to think about at this point if you are looking to grow, and one reason to hone in on that 50,000 subscriber number.

First, you absolutely will have to have paid acquisition channels at this point. Whether it's Facebook Ads, Sparkloop, conventions, or some combination of channels, you need ways to keep filling both your financial coffers and your subscriber count. It's critical at this point that you have a self-liquidating offer that allows you to keep scaling your ads by offering new subscribers a course or other modality so you can recoup those costs quickly. Usually, this is a $27-$37 course of some type that people buy with enough frequency to completely or mostly pay for the ad costs associated with running them.

I'm at this stage now, and it's harrowing. I'm spending $5,000-$10,000/mo on ads, and it keeps me up at night. Even with a self-liquidating offer, it's so much money I can't even keep it in my head. It doesn't help that the offer is unreliable at this stage, so I'm freaking out about it.

However, I'm growing very fast, and I want to reach that number for one reason. Elite publications in most fields have at least 50,000 subscribers, and if you're looking to monetize sponsorships or advertising, most people won't be interested until you get at least 50,000 subscribers.

At this point, you're probably capping out at what you can earn from your one channel, and it's time to start expanding to other monetization paths. The more monetization paths and price points you have, the more subscribers you need to support them. I'm looking to find enough subscribers that I can sell out our conference in 1-2 emails.

Once you reach this stage, your network has leveled up a ton, and you will have access to all sorts of interesting collaborations that can change your life with the snap of a finger.

Phase 6—50,000-100,000 subscribers

At this point, you're expanding your business and success paths quickly, ramping them up more and more as you get more subscribers. You're probably at a Level 5 by the time you reach 50,000 (or even before), but you will definitely be there at 100,000 subscribers. This is also the point you'll absolutely want to start looking at expanding your team. You probably should have built out your team at the previous stage, but you'll certainly need people who specialize in other areas besides you so that you can focus on your zone of genius.

Phase 7—100,000-1,000,000+ subscribers

By this point, you are one of the elite newsletters in your niche and are almost certainly pulling in at least six, if not seven, figures a year. Nearly nobody gets above 50,000 subscribers, and even fewer get to 100,000, especially not without a lot of work. You've made a name for yourself both in your industry and the overall newsletter game if you hit these numbers.

However, you need to realize this whole thing only works if your newsletter is engaged.

I've tried to scale 3x in my career, and every time I hit 25,000, my opens plateaued. I've had as many as 75,000 people on my mailing list, but I was still not getting any more opens than when I had 20,000.

Yes, your open rate will go down as you scale because that's just what happens when you start adding a lot of new people to your ecosystem, but if you start getting to the point where your opens aren't going up, then you need to stop and reevaluate.

The metric I look at most is WAU (weekly active users). If that number is going up, then I'm happy. If it stays flat or goes down, then I have to make adjustments. When you're playing at this level, any mistake can cost thousands of dollars, so I try to track these things very carefully.

***

With Sparkle—My goal is 10k subscribers. I'm nearly at 7k now and $35k GAR. The growth, for me, is about depth—depth of connection with my subs and members, depth of support, and setting new boundaries so I can support as many people as possible to stay creative on Substack.

***

Final thoughts

The reason I broke these out the way I did is because there is an intense and fundamental mindset shift that blocks people from jumping from one stage to the next. At the first stage, it's about wanting to do it all themselves or failing to put in the work to show up.

At stage 2, it's about selling to other writers instead of networking with them. At stage 3, it's about the fear of shedding things even if they aren't working. At stage 4, it's about fearing paid acquisition channels. At stage 5, it's about expanding your team with quality people instead of cheap labor.

I've been stuck at most of these stages before, and it was only fundamentally breaking those mental barriers that got me past them, but it's scary. It's so, so, so scary because there's almost always money on the line, and you have to spend it before you make it.

Why (and how) to do a roundup

I (Russell) talked to a very nice human recently who told me they already have a roundup of things they like but weren't highlighting people in their industry doing work on Substack.

So, in short, they missed the point.

The point of a roundup is to create community and highlight other people on Substack that your readers should also read to help you grow your network and your publication.

Or, if you want to grow on Facebook, Linkedin, or wherever, then who's doing work on that platform instead?

You should be sharing articles by people working either at your level, above or below you. Then, everyone in your industry will want to subscribe so they can stay informed on the important news of the day and connect around them.

Sorry if this breaks the illusion of what I'm doing. It's super strategic and a giveback to the community because things can be more than one thing, and they should be if you want to create leverage in your business.

You can't just share the biggest stories because everyone will likely have already seen those. You also have to become good at finding the hidden gems everyone needs to read but aren't getting enough attention.

This is how you can shine a spotlight on smaller publications. People really want to read those articles, by the way. Those are the ones I hear about all the time. I rarely hear about the viral ones because everyone's already read them.

If you create a roundup with the best articles you have read surrounding your publication's topic and also tag the people who wrote them, they will see that you care about the same things they do, that you care about their work, that you have good taste, and that you are a cool person who deserves their attention.

Then, they will be more open to letting you into their bubble.

If you keep doing it for months and years, it will all build on itself, even if you don't do anything else. Newsletters have made a killer eight-figure business on nothing but this concept.

As more and more people connect with you, it creates a virtuous cycle that amplifies everyone, including you.

STILL, YOU MUST ANNOUNCE YOUR PRESENCE.

You have to announce yourself subtly, but you need a way to show that you see them. That's a big reason why you are tagging them, so they get a subtle ping that you noticed them. At every level, people like to feel seen and know their work matters.

That said, you can't do this in a cheap way. People can sniff out a gimmick a mile away. I really, really care about every article I share. I believe in everything I put into my weekly roundup, but I also do it with intention.

Your goal is to connect with people whose work you authentically love and who you're happy to promote. You should be promoting people in your little corner of the internet and trying to amplify their voices.

If you do it in silence, there's no reason to have a roundup unless you really want one. Then, you do whatever you want. Still, it will almost certainly be better if more people know about it.

Aside from improving your writing, being a good curator is probably the best skill you can develop, and being a good connector is an art that can give you a career faster than anything else if you do it well.

Not everyone will appreciate it, but some people will, and it will be enough. Luckily, it's relatively easy to make a roundup part of your routine. So, let's talk about how to do that.

The good news is that there's almost no wrong way to do a roundup. Personally, my favorite roundup is *Today in Tabs*. They write their newsletters like a story and add links as they go to build them. I find it so charming and engaging that I don't even mind that they include a thousand links in every post.

As you can imagine, what I love about it is that there is a story. Yes, there are a hundred links and tags, but you can read it without clicking any of them and have a great time doing it. While mine is not a complete clone, it was the inspiration for how I do a roundup. Hopefully, you get a smile or a chuckle reading it.

I have found that because I like to send out a lot of links, it works better to write in a format that's a little more entertaining than a standard roundup. There seems to be no upper limit of links people will accept as long as they are entertained.

Another popular option is what *Today in Books* does with theirs, choosing articles and doing write-ups of them.

This is the traditional Morning Brew method of writing a digest. *Morning Brew* was a pioneer in the daily newsletter space, creating daily emails that can be easily consumed in a couple of minutes by anyone.

If you're a Desert, then this method probably resonates with you a lot. It's also the easiest to train somebody to mimic. Personally, I like to have more personality in my work, which means it won't resonate with as many people but will resonate more deeply with the people who do connect with it.

One of my favorites that sits at the intersection of these is Roxane Gay's roundups for her publication *The Audacity*. You can also choose to do a roundup for only paid subscribers, which is what Emma Gannon does with the *Sunday Scrolls*.

One thing I do recommend is consistency. It's always a good idea to set expectations early. When I started, my main newsletter was called *7 Cool Things*, based on the *5-Bullet Friday* method developed by Tim Ferris, which is almost exactly what it sounds like: a roundup of five cool things he found that week.

One of the best examples of this on Substack is the newsletter run by Austin Kleon. Every week, they send out ten interesting things they found worth sharing.

Of course, Substack does this with their *Weekly Stack*, an email they send out with personalized recommendations. They also run all sorts of digests through their *Substack Reads* newsletters. Most notable is their weekly roundup of the most interesting articles on Substack.

As you can see, like Snickers, there's almost no wrong way to eat one. However, whatever you choose, you should maintain consistency. For my own, I like to open with a little update on my life and a photo that will act as the main image.

Then, I will ask for a poll to gauge how people are doing. I follow up with any important notes or books that are launching. The next section I put in every newsletter is "What we wrote", which highlights every article launched during the week.

Then, I mention anywhere I've been interviewed during the week, followed by a snippet of next week's article.

Then comes the roundup, broken into three sections: Business-y, Publishing-like, and Culture-ish.

I set up my roundups like this because I expect it to be the most-read article in my publication every week. I set it up in its own section so that readers can unsubscribe from every other section and only read this one piece to get all the news they need to know. When you write multiple articles a week, it's very important to allow options for your readers only to get the work they want to read.

I'm also just...very busy. This allows me to talk about everything going on with me at one time. Whether they want to know what's up with me, what's up with my work, or what's up on Substack, I want to deliver something everyone can enjoy.

One final note. I can't do this alone. I rely on other creators I trust to share interesting articles, and lead me down fun rabbit holes when it comes to finding what to share with readers. Additionally, I look at the virality of a piece to see if it warrants inclusion. Sometimes, I pass on a piece, but then it gets shared a hundred times. I see how it's resonating with people as they share snippets, and I grow to understand why it's important.

***

With Sparkle—Make it shareable. I started a community-building project called *Sparkle* on Substack Essay Club to share accountability and give myself content to share on Notes and in roundups.

I share one roundup of the essays a season and get tagged in essays every single day.

Essay Club is a space to build accountability, gamify the system (there's a badge), and keep folks showing up to the keyboard and for their writing.

The original post has 4300 views and drove 70 new subs to Sparkle on Substack.

At the time of writing, it's two months old, and new people find it every week because the original people who saw it link to it. I also co-authored a call out for 'Substack Love' with a writer and content creator called Kat River. People could share their favorite Substack articles in the comments, and we curated them and pinged them all around. In the end, this was a lot of work, but it was beautiful work. Because my readers 'miss' things, I also do a monthly roundup of just my posts and replays, and this always drives new free and paid subs.

***

How to use Substack sections to strengthen your backlist and give subscribers even more value

I (Russell) have dozens of different Substack sections. Some might say I have a hoarding problem, but there's a very, very good reason for me to have so many. ***It's because I'm a hoarder.***

No, the real reason is that I recently learned that when somebody clicks a link to unsubscribe from your Substack, they are brought to a page where, in addition to completely unsubscribing, they can slide on and off the sections that interest them.

It's marketing gold, and you don't even have to do much except set up and populate the sections.

Segmenting and personalization are very important to me. I've had a newsletter for years, and while I don't have different sections inside of it, I allow people to choose how often they get emails from me. It has significantly reduced the number of unsubscribes I get to any email and improved the overall user experience.

This is even better.

I have been trying to find a way to make subscriptions work in my business for a long time.

I've even gone so far as to license my app...to disastrous results. I don't think I made 10% of the costs back on it after a year. It was brutal, but I persisted because I believe having a membership is part of the future of publishing.

The problem with subscription platforms like Patreon up until now is that the only legitimate way to offer books to people was to upload PDFs or ebooks, and I am adamantly against that idea. It encourages people to subscribe for one month, download everything, and unsubscribe. ***I am not about that life.***

I have my books available for purchase on my website, but if people subscribe, I'm not comfortable giving them downloads if I can't restrict their access when they unsubscribe.

With Substack sections, I saw the perfect opportunity to upload my back catalog as a bonus for paid subscribers and serialize stories to find new readers. Meanwhile, I can deliver to everyone exactly what they want.

Functionally, this works when somebody goes to my main page and clicks on bonus stories.

They choose a newsletter, pick the chapter and start reading. When they're ready for the next chapter, they click and keep reading.

I have this book set up as a bonus for paid subscribers only, but I am also serializing one of my longer novel series every week, and new chapters are free for everyone.

You might ask, "But Russell, you have a nonfiction publication. Why would you mix the two audiences?"

The truth is that it's because...***well, I don't think it matters much***, especially if readers can personalize what they hear about from me.

I believe that ***every person contains multitudes***, and some percentage of people who read about building an author business want to read cool books. At the same time, some fiction readers often want to hear what authors think about their business. The methodology for segmenting your disparate writer lives from each other is algorithmic, anyway.

On retailers, you don't get a chance to segment your audience. They do it for you. ***Retailers are search engines.*** People looking for one book are likely going to check out other similar books, so keeping every pen name narrowly focused makes sense...but Substack doesn't work like that.

Substack is a much more intimate experience where people are much more likely to jump between a lot of your stuff. For instance, I recently launched a nonfiction book on Kickstarter, and even though my fiction email list is filled with readers, not authors, 13,000 of 20,000 people on my email list opened at least one email about it during the campaign.

That's right. ***65% of my fiction mailing list opened an email about nonfiction because it was me talking about the process of creating books.***

Now, they didn't all buy, ***not even close***, but there's way more cross-pollination than most industry experts would have you believe. Not to mention, ***even if they don't care about what I'm showing them...they can unsubscribe from just that section.***

Okay, if I haven't convinced you this might be a good idea by now, I never will. For those of you who want to learn more, I'm going to show you exactly how to do this for your own author business.

I'm going to break this into a few parts. **In PART 1,** I will show you how to create a section. **In PART 2**, I will show you how to set up a template. **In PART 3,** I will show you how to build each chapter.

Then, I added two bonus sections. **In the first section,** I will talk about how I got 25,000+ paid subscribers in less than two weeks. **In the second section,** I will walk you through how to optimize your publication for searchability and subscriber growth.

Part 1

Let's talk about setting up your new section.

Before you do this, you should decide how to categorize each new section. ***I chose to categorize first by series and then by recurring segments of my newsletter (like my weekly wellness thread).***

So, I have a 12-book series called The Godsverse Chronicles, and I chose to make that one section instead of 12 different books. I might have made a different choice if I wasn't going to serialize it for the next several years, but that is a choice you need to make, too.

STEP 1: Go into your dashboard and click on the settings.

STEP 2: Either scroll or click on SECTIONS in the left-hand menu.

STEP 3: Click on + ADD SECTION.

STEP 4: From here, you have some options. Fill out the title of your section. If you are uploading a complete book/story/section that won't be updated, then I recommend adding [**COMPLETE**] at the end so people can denote it easily. If you are going to keep updating it, then you can add [**ONGOING**].

Then, add your description. I like adding the tagline from my novel to that description field. You don't get a lot of space on the newsletter page, so I want to make it short and sweet.

For *The Vessel*, the tagline is: **A million years ago, the world ended. Since then, a group of five have kept the City running. Now, one of them has died.**

You will also want to upload a square image for the header. For *The Vessel*, I used a piece of the cover, but you can also use DepositPhotos to find a cool picture like I did with *My Father Didn't Kill Himself*.

You'll also need a 16x9 image of the same, or similar, photo to use in the updates. ***We'll use this for the chapter images.*** You can use different imagery for each chapter, but that seems to complicate an already tedious process, so I chose one image for everything to ensure brand consistency.

STEP 5: You'll have to make three final decisions on this page: *Whether to hide posts from your homepage, whether to automatically add people to your new section*, and *whether to copy your current email list into the new section.*

Because I want to make my main Substack nonfiction specific, ***I chose to hide posts for my fiction*** from it, so all of my other newsletters are mostly hidden from my main page to keep it clean. ***These are bonuses, after all.***

Additionally, I have a weekly wellness thread that I chose to keep hidden as well, as I don't think it adds much to the aesthetic of the page. I won't hide these tutorials from the page, though. ***This is what I meant above by categorizing recurring segments.*** I didn't add [ONGOING] to these recurring segments since they aren't stories or books.

While I don't add new subscribers to completed stories, I do automatically add them to the weekly wellness thread, these tutorials, and my ongoing stories.

Copying your current subscribers is also a really important question because you can't change your mind. There currently is no functionality inside Substack to add subscribers to a section after you have imported them.

This actually happened to me. I created a section and didn't copy over my list, only to regret it later. ***I had to create a brand new section that copied everyone over*** and then change the section on every post manually. It took a while, but it did work out in the end. I'll show you how to do that below.

Just like with automatically adding people, ***I chose not to copy people to completed stories, but I decided to copy them to ongoing sections, both in fiction and nonfiction.***

STEP 6: Click CREATE SECTION, and you're ready to go.

Please note that Substack automatically creates a new top menu item for your new section, so if you're going to do a bunch of sections, you probably want to hide it by either scrolling up to the WEBSITE section (or clicking it on the left menu) and clicking the eye on the right side of the navigation to hide it.

STEP 7 (*optional*): While in the WEBSITE section of the menu, HIDE the /newsletters link and CREATE A NEW LINK to /newsletters with a fun name like BONUS STORIES by clicking + NEW LINK at the bottom of the list.

NOTE: You can't change the name of the original newsletters link, but you can create a new one with a different name and link it to the same place.

STEP 8 (*optional*): If you want to go the extra mile, then instead of creating a link to your /newsletters page, then you can create a brand new page on your publication to showcase all your sections like I have done for both fiction and nonfiction.

To set this up, go to DASHBOARD>SETTINGS>WEBSITE>+ NEW PAGE.

STEP 9 (*optional*): Once you have your new page, you can set it up just like any other article. I recommend a title like [X TYPE OF BOOK] AVAILABLE ON [YOUR PUBLICATION].

STEP 10 (*optional*): Once you are done, I would add a divider to separate the header from the different sections. Then, I should separate by genre (like fantasy) and add an image, the title, the subgenre, whether it's ongoing, and whether it's free or paid. I recommend looking at The Link Library for a good format.

STEP 11 (*optional*): Once you've done that, put your blurb, a link to the section, and then a link to buy the book *(if you have one).*

Continue doing this for every section to keep a running tally of all your sections in one convenient place for readers.

If you think this option is nonsense busywork, then you are in the right mindset for this whole exercise.

Yay! You've created your section. Now, let's populate it.

You aren't even close to done, but this cute mashup makes you feel a little bit of happiness, right?

Part 2

Let's talk about setting up a template inside your section. This is not the only way to set it up, but after studying a bunch of fiction and nonfiction Substacks, I found that this worked for me.

STEP 1: Click on NEW POST.

STEP 2: Choose your SECTION. This will likely be the biggest change for you. Once you have more than one section, this menu dropdown will appear on the top left side of your editor. ***NOTE: If you delete your section, then everything will revert to the main publication section.***

STEP 3: Choose your author. If you have more than one author, you will have to choose this every time you duplicate a post, which you will be doing a lot in this part.

STEP 4: Add your title. For ongoings, I add the names of the books, like Magic - Chapter 8. For complete stories, I say Chapter 1, Episode 1, or Issue 1. Since everything is in its own section and nobody is going to get an email, it shouldn't be confusing. The only difference is for things like *My Father Didn't Kill Himself,* which is epistolary, so I chose to add the blog post title in the headline, and for nonfiction books, which I broke up into relevant sections like MAKING GREAT CONTENT, so readers can find the extract they need.

STEP 5: Add your subtitle. For the first chapter, I use the tagline I used for the description. For each subsequent chapter, I use the first non-spoiler line from the chapter I can find.

So, for *The Vessel*, the subtitle for Chapter 1 is, ***A million years ago, the world ended. Since then, a group of five have kept the City running. Now, one of them has died***, just like the newsletter description. However, the subtitle for Chapter 2 is, ***I shouldn't have said anything. I should have left like a thief in the night, but I couldn't do it. I needed them to know I was going.***

STEP 6: Now, we're going to create the template for your section. That way, all you have to do is ***duplicate into draft*** and save a ton of time.

So, the first thing I do when making a template is take that big, beautiful SQUARE image we made for the section and put it at the top of the page so the first thing readers see is the image.

Make sure you have the right to do this from your cover designer or have them do it for you.

STEP 7: Now, go to MORE in the toolbar and drop in a divider. This is going to denote your header section from the chapter text. I also like to format my headers in bold to separate them from the rest of the post.

This is my header for *The Vessel.*

The Vessel is a dystopian science fiction in the style of Hunger Games, Divergent, or Maze Runner. You can find more of my work on my website.

A million years ago, the world ended. Since then, a group of five have kept the City running. Now, one of them has died.

Every generation, the five most powerful people in the City transfer their consciousnesses into nubile teenage hosts. This allows them to continue their important work of keeping the City functioning and protected from the nuclear wasteland beyond its borders.

When one of the Five dies, though, the others decide that their bodies are too fragile and decide to find new hosts earlier than usual. This triggers a competition, where children from across the City travel to its center to compete for a chance to earn a place as a Vessel for one of the Five.

If chosen, their families will be taken care of for the rest of eternity. There is great prestige in being a Vessel, along with enormous wealth for the families of the chosen, which means every participant has their own motivations for competing.

Althea is one of those competitors. She is from a poor farming family on the outskirts of the City, and with the money she receives from her sacrifice, her family would never have to work again. She is willing to risk her life for them.

So, she decides to compete, traveling from her home in the outer rings through the inner rings and finally to the center where the competition is held.

Along the way, she discovers the City she once venerated is a more dangerous place than she ever thought possible. Every turn is fraught with peril, and the competition could be the death of her, even if she doesn't win.

Join Althea for a story of friendship, love, struggle, and perseverance in the face of enormous odds. Perfect for anybody who loved Divergent, The Hunger Games, or The Maze Runner.

Paid subscribers can access the entire archive of this series from the beginning, along with other series and every article I've ever written. If you aren't a paid subscriber, you can access the archive for free with a 7-day trial.

Let's break this down a bit more.

The Vessel is a dystopian science fiction in the style of Hunger Games, Divergent, or Maze Runner. You can find more of my work on my website.

The first thing I want to do is tell or remind the reader what kind of story they are reading and then give them a way to find more. You might instead want to send them to your newsletter page or somewhere else.

A million years ago, the world ended. Since then, a group of five have kept the City running. Now, one of them has died.

Every generation, the five most powerful people in the City transfer their consciousnesses into nubile teenage hosts. This allows them to continue

their important work of keeping the City functioning and protected from the nuclear wasteland beyond its borders.

When one of the Five dies, though, the others decide that their bodies are too fragile and decide to find new hosts earlier than usual. This triggers a competition, where children from across the City travel to its center to compete for a chance to earn a place as a Vessel for one of the Five.

If chosen, their families will be taken care of for the rest of eternity. There is great prestige in being a Vessel, along with enormous wealth for the families of the chosen, which means every participant has their own motivations for competing.

Althea is one of those competitors. She is from a poor farming family on the outskirts of the City, and with the money she receives from her sacrifice, her family would never have to work again. She is willing to risk her life for them.

So, she decides to compete, traveling from her home in the outer rings through the inner rings and finally to the center where the competition is held.

Along the way, she discovers the City she once venerated is a more dangerous place than she ever thought possible. Every turn is fraught with peril, and the competition could be the death of her, even if she doesn't win.

Join Althea for a story of friendship, love, struggle, and perseverance in the face of enormous odds. Perfect for anybody who loved Divergent, The Hunger Games, or The Maze Runner.

Next, I drop in the blurb for the book. I do this every time in case people get drawn away into some other task and need a reminder when they finally sit down again.

Finally, I pitch them on becoming a paid subscriber and give them a way to start from the beginning of the story just in case they found the wrong page.

CRITICAL NOTE: Make sure all the links work properly before you move on. If the links don't work, you'll have to fix them individually, which could take hours. I know from experience. Test those links NOW!**

STEP 8: Add an easy way for them to join. I have studied a bunch of Substacks, and these three were what resonated with me.

I put it at the top of every page, including this one.

STEP 9: Now, let's go to the footer.

The Vessel is a dystopian science fiction in the style of Hunger Games, Divergent, or Maze Runner. You can find more of my work on my website.

Paid subscribers can access the entire archive of this series from the beginning, along with other series and every article I've ever written. If you aren't a paid subscriber, you can access the archive for free with a 7-day trial.

You'll see this is almost identical to the header, without the blurb, since they already know the story. ***This duplication process is why you must check your links in the header FIRST before you move on to do anything else.***

STEP 10: Now, go to the CONTINUE button in the top right corner of the page. Choose whether this will be for free or paid subscribers, and then choose **UPLOAD NEW** in the imagery. This is where you are going to upload that 16x9 image you made before.

While the main image for a section is SQUARE, the imagery for each post inside a section is rectangular. It's not quite 16x9 either, but that framing still worked for me because I don't know the right size. Again, ***you can choose a different image for each chapter, but I wasn't willing to make that kind of commitment to sourcing imagery.***

STEP 11 (optional): This is also where you can make changes to your social preview and search engine optimization text. Perhaps you want a different title for your SEO, your social preview, and your actual post. This is where you can make those changes.

The social preview is immediately editable. If you want to edit the SEO options, then you need to click the triangle pointing to the right in the SEO Options box, which will expand it.

This is also when you can change the POST URL to shorten it or make it more precise for your needs.

STEP 11: Uncheck anything at the bottom that says "SEND TO..." so that it just says publish now, and then publish. This is just a shell we are using as a template, so we don't want ANYONE to see it yet.

STEP 12: Hit publish. Now, you have a template. Let's create a finished post now.

This takes intense, tedious focus and attention to detail. Fun times!

Part 3

We'll now add to this template and flush out a full post from it.

STEP 1: Go to the dashboard and right-click the three dots on the right side of your template. Then, click **DUPLICATE TO DRAFTS**.

Every time you need a new chapter, you can use this method. For the completed story, you should plan on creating the whole book before you start publishing it (***I'll show you why later***). For ongoing stories, I recommend 10 posts before you start promoting them so that people can get hooked on your world.

STEP 2: Open your Word document and decide how long you want each "chapter" to be for each post. Maybe you're willing to upload every chapter for every book, but I don't have time for that.

I do think it matters that readers have a consistent post length throughout your book, but you can choose the length that works for you. My general rule for posts is five chapters or roughly 5,000 words for completed books. It's good to have at least 10 chapters in each section, but it feels overwhelming to have 80. So, roughly five chapters ended up working out for me.

NOTE: I only made this choice for completed stories. For ongoing, I chose to go chapter by chapter.

STEP 3: Once you have copied the length that feels right to you, paste it ***between*** the header and footer.

STEP 4 (*optional*): Make sure the paragraph formatting is right. You might paste your document and see that everything is indented. You can make your choice, but I chose to format my fiction books like a Substack post, so if there was an indentation, I deleted it manually. I think it makes everything look crisp and uniform.

STEP 5 (***optional***): Strip out all chapter and scene breaks and replace them with something pretty. I went to DepositPhotos and found pretty vector imagery that acted as scene breaks for each book.

Since I was combining multiple book chapters into one Substack CHAPTER, it didn't make sense for it to say "chapter" a bunch of times, so I stripped all of that out and replaced it with a pretty image.

If this sounds like a lot of tedious work, you're right. I should have probably had a PA do it, but I don't mind tedious work. I find it calming in a way.

STEP 6: Once you have the formatting right, you need to add **READ THE NEXT CHAPTER** at the end of it and add a link to the next chapter.

How do you get the link? This is why it's a good idea to duplicate the drafts for all chapters at once.

Head back to the dashboard and go into the **NEXT CHAPTER DRAFT** in the drafts. For instance, if you're currently working on Chapter 1, then open Chapter 2.

Once you are inside the draft, click the settings at the bottom right. Look for the **SECRET DRAFT LINK**. Copy it and open your original chapter draft. You can also expand the SEO Options and set, then copy the POST URL.

Note: Anyone you share this link with will be able to view this draft even if it has not been published. Reset the link if you'd no longer like them to have access.

Now, go back to the previous chapter. Highlight the **READ NEXT CHAPTER** and add the link to the **NEXT CHAPTER** inside your current chapter.

In the **FINAL CHAPTER** of a completed work, I like to add **FIND SOMETHING NEW TO READ** instead of READ NEXT CHAPTER with a link to my NEWSLETTERS page.

If this sounds tedious, then you're right! Now rinse and repeat. I'll bet you're happy to have a template now, right?

If you don't want to do this tediousness, you can go to DASHBOARD>SETTINGS>WEBSITE>ENABLE PREVIOUS & NEXT POST LINKS.

STEP 7: Once you have all your drafts compiled, it's time for final checks. Open them all and look for:

1. Is your section correct?
2. Is your chapter right?
3. Is your subtitle good?
4. Does your link to the next chapter redirect properly?
5. Did you make any egregious mistakes in the heading or footer?

STEP 8: If you have a completed story, publish it in ***reverse*** order. So, if you have 10 different posts, start at 10 and go backward to 1. Why? So it looks right on the section page. Otherwise, 10 will show up first instead of 1.

If you have an ongoing one, then publish them in the normal order.

STEP 9: Go into your dashboard, click the three dots on CHAPTER 1, and click PIN ON [SECTION NAME].

STEP 10: Check your homepage to make sure everything is hidden (or at least looks right).

STEP 11: Duplicate your template into drafts so you can use it as the basis for your next section, and delete the template so it doesn't show up in your section.

STEP 12 (*optional*): Go into your first chapter and share it with your email list.

STEP 13 (*optional*): This might be a good time to unhide your NEWSLETTERS tab in the website section (if you ever turned it off).

STEP 14: Starting with Chapter 1, click through the whole story and make sure all the links work one last time.

STEP 15 (*optional*): Submit your new book to The Library and start connecting with other people in your genre for some cross-promotion.

You've done it! Woot! Let's celebrate!

***

With Sparkle—I'm also a HUGE fan of sections. I set up a secret section and subscribed to one so I could test how that all worked in the back office...it worked. No one saw those posts, but I could like them.

***

Bonus section #1:

If you decide to play this game, then you're probably looking for ways to maximize eyeballs on your work for all the hours you'll spend on it. So, as promised, this is how I got 25,000+ paid subscribers to my Substack in under two weeks.

The secret? ***I comped my whole email list with a free 3-month trial.***

I know that's a sneaky trick to get you to read this far, but I also know there are people writers there with big email lists and have never even thought about bringing them over. So, ***this is how I did it and why.***

I have 20,000 people on my fiction email list and close to 5,000 on our Writer MBA list. Both those mailing lists had become hyper-focused on promotions and launches without offering that much value-based content. I wanted to change that and make more posts like these.

Except I ***was*** making them...***I was just making them here on Substack.*** On top of that, I was writing specifically for the exact kind of people who were already on our mailing lists. Our best stuff is behind a paywall in our membership, but the next best is made right here.

It made complete sense to bring all of them to Substack (*I can't overstress that these were people who had already opted-in to our lists*). Once we made that decision, the question became how could I shower them with love and attention so they got excited to get more emails from me. If you haven't guessed, I'm a tundra, so ***excitement is my superpower.***

Here are some things I considered and how I thought through them.

1. I already had people unsubscribe from my paid Substack subscription, citing a lack of content, so I had to be hyperfocused on delivering tons of value. Because of our extensive network of courses, I was able to offer $50+ in free courses to new members from the beginning, but that still wasn't enough for some paid

subscribers. So, I decided to upload almost my entire back catalog of solo nonfiction and fiction books to Substack so people could see the value immediately. My audience is made up of authors and other creators, fantasy readers, and comics fans. So, I catered our bonus content to excite each segment. I uploaded multiple fantasy novels, almost my entire comic library, and my collection of solo nonfiction books. Plus, I added some mystery and science fiction novels into the mix as well. I made sure to service all of them with something meaty that I thought would pique their interest.

2. Then, I strategically decided to increase my weekly output. My posts are long and complicated. They pull on many disciplines and have dozens of links. So, I couldn't commit to another one of those, but I could do a weekly round-up post of my favorite Substacks (*I read hundreds*) and serialize one of my series without much extra work. It takes me about 30 minutes to make my weekly roundup post and maybe 30 minutes to schedule my serializations for the month, and that already tripled my output in less than an hour a week. Both my weekly wellness post and my serialized novels are in their own sections that people can unsubscribe to individually if they don't want to see those posts.
3. Once I had those two things in place, I needed to give subscribers a reason to check it out by paywalled content, which is why we comped everyone already on my list with a three-month paid membership. I needed them to feel like this was a big perk, not a burden, so giving them something that had tangible value made sense. *I find that people get excited about getting more content from you and less so about getting more promotions from you.* Substack is all value. *Now, I have three months to show them that value.* Can I do it? I don't know, but I have done everything I can to make it worthwhile for them. Maybe 10% of people will get excited to continue their membership, or maybe 10 will, but I feel confident that I've delivered as much value as I can to demonstrate that it's not a waste of time. Now, I just have to prove it.

I talked before about breaking my year up into quarters and testing one thing per quarter. It took a little longer to set this up than I would have liked, but this is my second quarter test. How long did it take? ***About two weeks of full-time work to get everything uploaded and formatted properly***. That sounds like a lot of time, but I never have to upload them again, and it will (hopefully) keep delivering value for years to come. Remember, ***I have nineteen sections to coordinate. Your time will vary.***

I should note that in my experience, ***three months is the minimum amount of time it takes to find significant value in my work***. We don't even offer monthly pricing for our membership for that reason.

If you're interested in doing this with your own Substack, here's the breakdown of how to make this happen.

STEP 1: Before you do this, ***make sure to send an email to your list telling them what to expect and wait at least one week to import them into Substack.*** Even if you do this step perfectly, a few subscribers will complain, but loading them into Substack without warning will be much worse. Plus, for those few who do complain, you can always direct them back to the email you sent setting expectations.

NOTE: ***Don't forget to update your Substack welcome emails with any new information your new subscribers need to know about their special bonuses.***

STEP 2: Pull down a CSV from your current email service provider. Scrub out anyone who has unsubscribed before uploading to Substack. Please make sure they opted-in to your list and follow CAN-SPAM, GDPR, or whatever governs your region. Also, only even consider this if you actively update your subscribers regularly, not if you've had a dead list for a year.

I would also strongly consider only bringing people over who have opened an email from you in the last 3-6 months. Otherwise, your open rates will likely crater. I forgot to do this for the last 9,000 emails I moved over, and my open rates were cut nearly in half after I added them.

STEP 3: Delete everything but the emails from the .csv file. **It does need to be a .csv to upload properly.**

STEP 4: Go to your dashboard and click on subscribers on the top menu.

STEP 5: Click **ADD SUBSCRIBERS**.

STEP 6: Drag your CSV into **ADD EMAILS BY UPLOADING A CSV FILE** and drop.

STEP 7: A pop-up will appear.

Choose the length of time you want to give subscribers a trial. I think three months is a good amount of time for readers to get settled and extract significant value from a membership. Decide whether you want to give existing free subscribers a free trial (*I did*) and whether you want to send a welcome email (*I did*).

Then, quickly explain where these emails came from, especially if it's a big list. Then, confirm that these people opted in and import.

NOTE: It is critical that you have your sections set up properly. It's probably worth double-checking to make sure your "AUTOMATICALLY ENROLL" and "COPY SUBSCRIBERS" options are right in the section settings. If it's not, then there's no way to fix it later, even manually.

STEP 8 (*optional*): Once the trial period is over, go into your SUBSCRIBERS tab and FILTER out the people who haven't opened anything from you and chose not to continue their subscription.

The filters I recommend are:

- Subscription type ***IS*** free.
- Activity ***IS*** one unshaded star.
- Emails opened (last six months) ***IS*** zero.
- Email opens (last six months) ***IS*** zero.

- Post views (last six months) ***IS*** zero.
- Link clicks ***IS*** zero.
- Shares ***IS*** zero.

STEP 9 (***optional***): I consider these dead emails, or at least emails that have no interest in what I'm doing on Substack, so I want to make sure they aren't getting anything they don't want. So, it's time to cull these people.

Once you have filtered everything, click the box above the first subscriber to check everyone, and then click on **SELECT ALL [XXX].**

STEP 10 (***optional***): Click the THREE DOTS next to EMAIL, and then REMOVE.

The reason I used these filters is because (I think) it shows people who don't have a Substack account (hence the unshaded star in the activity) and who have never engaged with any content behind our paywall. If you send emails to people who don't engage, service providers are more likely to send your emails to the promotions tab or label them as spam.

I want to give them enough time to engage, though, which is why I comped everyone a three-month subscription instead of a one-week subscription. ***If somebody can't even be bothered to engage with one post during that time, then they will never see value in being a free subscriber.***

Let me be clear. ***I have no problem with free subscribers.*** Most people will be on your list for free for years without ever buying anything from you, and that's great. I think it's amazing that anyone would ever want to hear from me at all. That they let me occupy a little piece of their brain space with my emails is incredible.

I tried to filter out people who actively subscribed through Substack as well because they chose to engage with my publication. However, ***if the people you imported aren't at least going to engage once during their free trial period, then you should probably just let them go.***

Notice that I'm not kicking people off my main email list with my other ESP. ***They are just being booted from Substack.*** If they choose to re-engage with this publication later, they are welcome to resubscribe then.

Also, notice, ***I will only kick off free subscribers.*** If somebody has never engaged but wants to give me money, they can stick around forever.

NOTE: When somebody unsubscribes as a COMP subscriber, they will only be downgraded to FREE when their subscription runs out. Meanwhile, they will remain on your list as a COMP subscriber until then and as a FREE subscriber afterward. Therefore, when a COMP subscriber unsubscribes, you need to go into your SUBSCRIBER dashboard and make sure they are actually deleted from your database. I received several emails about this, and it took forever to figure out what was going on.

This is a lot of work, but I currently have over 25,000 potential paid subscribers, so I am highly motivated to make them over the moon happy for the next couple of months, even if I will likely boot 10,000 of them once the trial is over for not engaging with this publication at all.

Bonus section #2: Can refreshing your publication really help you get new subscribers?

After doing this exercise, I followed the advice of several prominent Substack experts and redesigned my publication to maximize engagement and findability.

STEP 1: I went through and fixed my About page, so there's a very easy-to-follow first paragraph with the effect I'm trying to impart to the reader (agency in a world that too often feels like you have none).

I focused on my bio before and added my universal fantasy to the bottom. However, as several people pointed out and reminded me, people won't read until the bottom if they aren't hooked at the top. So, I made sure to add a big splashy image, and highlighted where I wanted to draw the eye.

STEP 2: I fixed the header of every post with updated language to make it more brand-consistent. You can do this at DASHBOARD>SETTINGS>PUBLICATION DETAILS>Email banner, header, and footer settings>EDIT.

Once there, you can decide how to introduce yourself in every email you send. Here's mine:

Hi, I'm USA Today bestselling fantasy author, editor, and publisher Russell Nohelty. I sit at the intersection of craft and commerce, helping writers navigate the sticky bit between writing something that lights them up inside and building an audience of superfans who adore their work.

STEP 3: I went through my archives and changed the headlines to be more SEO-able.

OLD HEADLINE: *Why whisks are a harbinger of doom for the future of humanity.*

NEW HEADLINE: *How to use technology and productivity hacks to reclaim your time for things that matter.*

The old headlines are great for email headlines, but they are less great for discoverability. They were fun, but nobody was going to search for those search terms. You can find Substack's guide to SEO right here.

I plan to send emails with the same punchy headlines moving forward and then optimizing them for SEO a few days after launch moving forward.

I should also add that it is possible to have a different headline in your article than in your SEO.

To make that change, you would need to edit a post and go to the settings button at the bottom right (*or click update in the top right*). From there, scroll down to Social Preview and change how you want it to appear on social networks. ***The bold text will be the title, and the regular text below will be the description.***

Once you have this set, open up the SEO options box below it. This is how it will appear in search results.

So, I guess technically, it's possible to have three different titles and descriptions. ***This is also how you change the post URL, FYI.***

STEP 4: I upgraded my sections from pointing to my newsletter sections to nonfiction and fiction pages I designed based on the format I saw at The Link Library. ***I showed you how to do this above, so I'm not going to rehash it here.***

BONUS: A very nice human told me about a bunch of free directories where you can list your newsletter. Some of these links are dead now, but I signed up for those that still worked and were relevant.

The result: After implementing these changes, I saw an immediate 50% increase in subscribers from the previous week. I talked to somebody the other day who was writing a travel memoir on Substack. She has dozens of mystery novels and asked if she should do something like this with her work.

I absolutely think that's a resounding yes, as long as you have a long-term strategy in place and are willing to "go all in" for a couple of months to really test it.

In her case, there will be some travel fans who find her work and love reading books and some mystery readers who love to travel. In both cases, some of her fans will probably get excited to join this new adventure. Who knows, maybe it will work so well that she'll start serializing a travel mystery novel on Substack.

I should note that ***my gross annualized revenue took a hit during this time because many of my paid subscribers were on the comped list***, but I am hoping that it easily rebounds in a couple of months as trials end and people see the value of becoming a paid subscriber.

Also, it's important to have more in the pipeline than you give away at launch so that people keep seeing the value. I have two more big series ready to serialize on Substack starting next year if this test works.

Finally, ***make sure you don't overcommit to more than you are able to give without burning out.*** I know I can deliver killer value to everyone here with just one post a week, but now, people can see exponentially more value without taking much more of my energy. It took a lot to set it up, but moving forward, it will take very little maintenance.

It might not be as "clean" as having multiple publications, but sometimes you have to compromise to exist harmoniously in this world, and this is the balance I've struck. It works for me. I hope it can work for you, too.

How to go paid on Substack without selling your soul

There are two main hurdles that writers will face in building their creative careers. The first is developing the ability to craft exceptional work with a distinct voice that is uniquely their own. The second is building a sustainable business that lights them up inside.

Most scholarship is devoted to the craft part of the writing business and abandons creative people to deal with the business part of their writing largely by themselves.

Since creative people are left on their own for this part, they have to rely on the sales and marketing activities that work for other businesses driven more by maximizing revenue than artistic fulfillment.

So, it comes as no surprise that so many writers have issues with "going paid" on Substack because it underlies an important tenet that has been drilled into our heads from a young age: *commodifying art taints the pursuit of truth and devalues the work...*

...or some such nonsense to that effect.

If you have no interest in getting paid for your work, that's your choice, but the idea that making money on your art devalues it is utter poppycock. Exchanging goods and services has been a bedrock of civilization since the dawn of humanity.

When I (Russell) dig down into it with creators, their core aversion to sales and marketing is not tied to the money itself but the commodification of their writing into just another widget in the capitalist infrastructure.

That belief is not nonsense. In fact, commodifying art can absolutely destroy the value proposition of the artist, which is often built on uniqueness and innovation.

Substack works because it is built on the belief that your voice is unique and people will find you specifically ***because*** you are specifically ***not*** a commodity.

However, writing does not have to be a commodity to make money. In fact, the decommodification of your work can be ***the exact reason*** that people line up to buy it.

If we can get over that mental hurdle, then there are several ways to sell a paid Substack that aligns with artistic values, such as *providing value to your community, creating unique experiences for your fans,* and *facilitating joy in people's lives.*

So, if you have ever felt icky about going paid, here are some of my best mindset shifts to get you into the right headspace to ***joyously*** provide more for your audience than they ever thought possible. How to go paid on Substack without selling your soul.

Not everyone will join you behind the paywall, and that's okay

Only a fractional share of people (**2%-10%**) who follow you will even consider going paid, so any effort should be focused not on alienating them but on creating an environment where people who want to join are overwhelmed with awesome.

There is a chapter in *This is NOT a Book* all about how guilt can't scale, but the general idea is that using guilt as a cudgel alienates your audience and turns them away from you. Guilt can work to influence buyers in the short term, but it feels terrible and does not create the type of long-term customers who will gladly pay for your work far into the future.

Instead, flip this on its head and turn your paid Substack into an unmissable party for your biggest fans. Shower those people behind your paywall with love and make them feel like they are part of the in-crowd for joining you.

Because most won't, and that's okay.

I have been sending newsletters for close to a decade, and no matter what I write, some small segment of people will unsubscribe from my list. I could give them a code to download a $100 Amazon gift card, and some people will still unsubscribe.

I have sent every type of email in the universe, from "I'm in the hospital" to "Buy my book", and they all get roughly the same number of unsubscribes from people who are done listening to me.

That's okay, because I don't write for them. I write for the people who ***want*** to hear my message. The more you can focus your attention on those people, the better you will be mentally.

That said, focusing exclusively on paid members misses a big bit of human psychology. Namely, a lot of people just want to see what you're up to, even if they don't buy your stuff.

We undervalue lurkers and looky-loos, but the truth is that most people won't buy from you. They might come to your party, but they won't pay for a ticket.

Many members of your immediate family won't even buy from you, and that's okay. I'm sure you don't frequent their businesses, either, or use their services, but you still like to be around them.

Most people you know won't buy from you, but that doesn't mean they aren't interested in your stuff. It doesn't mean they won't read your posts, see your emails, and just get a nice feeling that you exist.

I have had a bunch of people in my life who said something like, "I don't read your emails, but I like that they show up, so I know you still exist. It gives me a good feeling inside."

And that's cool, too. It doesn't even matter if they talk you up. This isn't a marketing thing, it's just nice as a human to be able to elicit that reaction from people whether they buy from you or not.

I am all about getting paid for your work, but not at the expense of people who just want to hang out. You don't have to snub the people who want to hang out to cater a great experience for your paid members. It's okay to shower love on everybody in different ways.

Additionally, just because somebody says "no" doesn't mean "no" forever. It just means "no" right now. There are all sorts of reasons people choose not to join you this minute, and many times, those people will eventually join you if you stay in your truth and don't try to guilt them into it.

***

With Sparkle—When I first launched Sparkle on Substack, my % paid subs was 10%. I thought I would aim to keep it there, but it didn't work. Part of the reason it didn't work was that other 'Substack educators' offer free education, and their annual membership is 1/3 of the price of mine.

The other part was that I showed up in service to creatives, which meant there was a ton of content out there for free. Once I pivoted to sharing less, my subs went up. Every now and again, I'll do a challenge for beginners, and my paid subs go down, not up, but this drives more traffic to my publication and more subscribers. It's not a ton more subscribers—I'm talking like 20/30 for tens of hours of work, but I want to do it.

People like value, but they don't need a ton of emails or more on their 'to-do' list—this just causes overwhelm.

***

Limit your ask to certain times a year, like a PBS pledge drive

Even though you can donate to PBS throughout the year, they push hard during certain times of the year with telethons, special bonuses, and an intense focus on showing the value they provide.

Similarly, even though you should offer your paid membership throughout the year, consider designing a "pledge drive" when you first go paid (with a sweet yearly discount for paid subscribers) to build the critical mass necessary to devote time to your membership. Offer special pins, prints, or other bonuses for people who join during this special time, and try to get other creators with similar audiences to create a fun experience with you.

The hardest part of running a membership for paid subscribers is that whether there is one person or a thousand people behind a paywall, you have to do the work.

Once you have the initial drive complete, plan regular events to gather new members and convert free subscribers to paid ones. This has the added benefit of reminding your paid members why they subscribed in the first place to lower churn.

One of the biggest problems creators have with going paid is that they feel like they always have to be on, but if you confine your ask to certain times of the year, then you can concentrate on the work of creating most of the year.

In fact, you can fold up a membership around a product launch, like a book. In our newest Kickstarter campaign, I am offering a yearly subscription to this publication for $75, which includes a copy of the book and a VIP call with me.

There is also a masterclass available for $150, which provides a two-hour live course on top of the other bonuses. We have offered this very successfully in the past as well.

Map out the value for subscribers

The easiest way to convince yourself that paid subscribers are getting value from their membership is to take out a piece of paper and create a value stack where your paid subscribers get at least a 10x return for their investment.

Most Substacks that I see have a $5/mo or $50/yr membership tier. I think we can all agree that if somebody will get $500 in value from a $50 investment, then that's a pretty amazing deal.

If you plan on a $50/yr membership, then you need to find a way to provide $500/yr of value to somebody who joins.

This might sound like an insurmountable amount, but when you break it down, value is everywhere.

For instance, let's say you have a blog about making awesome salads, and your value is providing easy-to-prepare healthy salads that taste great. I will literally share every salad post I find with my wife because we are always looking for good salads. Even in Los Angeles, we have a heck of a time finding great ones.

If you have this kind of blog, then how many hours are you saving the average person who now doesn't have to scour the internet looking for healthy alternatives every week? Colloquially, I would say that we spend at least one hour a week looking at recipes.

The median salary for a worker in the USA is $54,132, which is an hourly rate of around $27/hr. So, if your stated goal was to save paid subscribers at least 1 hour a week, that's a value of $1,404 right there over a year. Even if you take the federal minimum wage of $7.25, that's still a $377 value.

Then, can you provide a checklist, cheat sheets, a short audio/video/email course with best practices, compilation books of your best posts, or something you can create once and give people at launch? Or could you provide a meal planning guide to save even more time?

When people go paid on my Substack, they get access to several courses relevant to my audience's interests, including ***How to Build an Audience from Scratch, Write a Great Novel, 10x your Productivity***, and the archives from my long-running podcast ***The Complete Creative***, which I pulled down from everywhere in 2020, even if you only sign up for a 7-day free trial.

Depending on how you value those things, it could be $500 worth of value by itself.

Office hours, chats, and other experiences that are only available to paid subscribers are also a big value. For example, **if you provide access to yourself for an hour a month and you bill out at $200/hr, that's over $2,000 in value right there.**

When you ***stack*** this ***value*** up, it's easy to provide a lot of benefits to a subscriber.

Realize people want to support your work

Building a 10x value stack into your paid community is as much about changing your mindset as it is about exciting your audience. Once you are comfortable with the value you provide, your audience should fall in line behind you.

In fact, many of them are probably ready to support you just because they believe in your vision and want you to keep doing your best work.

For a while, I asked everyone who joined my paid Substack what they wanted to see from me, and the overwhelming response was, "I just want to support your work". It was such a unanimous response that I stopped asking people.

We forget or have never internalized that people who believe in our work want us to keep doing it. The more quickly we can put out our best work is as much for their benefit as it is for ours.

In fact, many people in your community probably feel guilty about having gotten so much value from you over the years and will welcome the ability to support you and your work. Fans, in general, are amazing and will surprise you in unexpected ways.

Don't forget to check your list twice, or maybe even a third time, for redundancy.

Make a list of all the things that going paid will enable you to do for your audience

Patreon used to have a nice feature that allowed a creator to set goals for their community. It's not available anymore, and that's a whole different platform. Even if it was, we can still use it as a model to think about how extra support will make your community's life better.

- ***What will an additional $1,000/mo in revenue allow you to do for your community?*** Can you provide an extra post for them every month? Will you be able to hire a copy editor to improve the quality of the content? Can you produce a podcast where you go more in-depth about certain subjects?

- ***What will that money allow you NOT to do?*** Will you be able to stop taking client work? Will you be able to cut back to part-time at your job? Will it allow you to hire a VA so you don't have to handle admin work?

- ***How will that extra time positively impact your community?*** If you have an additional 5, 10, or 20 hours a week, how much more could you accomplish for your community? Maybe you want to delight your audience with extra bonuses, or maybe it will just put you in a better mental place to create your best work.

The intersection of art and commerce is really the intersection of artist and community.

Your community pays to receive what you have made and provides you the ability to create the next thing. Your receipt of their money allows you to continue delighting them with your work and create from a place of joy instead of fear.

It is a gift you are giving each other.

Look what I made for you.

At the end of the day, commerce and art are not at odds with each other. They are, instead, as intrinsically connected as the link between product and customer.

Every time I release something new, I start by saying, "Look at what I made for you".

I believe that deep in my soul. **I create little presents for their enjoyment.** Their patronage allows me to create even more for them. Everything I make is written with one human from my audience in mind. It is usually my wife, but it is nearly as often somebody else who I think will enjoy it.

Many artists have told me over the years that they think an adversarial relationship between art and commerce is a good thing, and I strongly disagree.

For years, I had an adversarial relationship with exercise, and because of that, I remained unhealthy. My mindset was such that I equated exercise to bad. It took changing my mindset so that I found joy in exercise before I was able to find something that worked for me.

Now, I exercise every day.

In the same way, if you have an adversarial relationship with commerce, then you will never be able to find joy in allowing your most ardent fans to pay you properly for the work you create.

Power, authority, and systems of oppression, yes, I think art should probably be adversarial to those things in many cases, but commerce does not have to exist inside those systems.

The most utopian of communes still have some form of commerce, even if it relies exclusively on bartering.

You create your relationship with money and boundaries for yourself and your community within that relationship. It can absolutely be an adversarial or parasitic relationship, but it can be a symbiotic one, too, that fills you with joy if you create it that way.

I have been coaching writers for close to a decade, and when they have an adversarial relationship with commerce, they, by and large, have trouble making a sustainable career from their work. In the worst cases, they end up sabotaging themselves repeatedly to prevent their success.

If you don't want to build a sustainable career, do whatever you want, but if you want this to be more than a hobby, then you have to find a way to make peace with commerce.

Selling your work doesn't have to destroy your soul, but we have to set our lives up in a way to protect ourselves and our audience to prevent that from happening.

If we can do that, then there is great joy in allowing somebody to give you money for something they will treasure forever.

What it really means to get that pretty orange checkmark

On Friday, August 25, at 9:12 AM, I (Russell) got the email most of us have been striving for and became a Substack bestseller.

What does that really mean, though?

Well, first off, I actually became a Substack bestseller the day before, and as far as I can tell, you don't actually need 101 paying members to receive bestseller status. All you need are 101 people who have agreed to either a trial membership, to start paying once their upgrade period is over, or to generate at least $1 in revenue from somebody without them canceling their membership.

At the time I received my orange checkmark, I had no less than 20 subscribers who hadn't paid me even $1. How is that possible?

Eight of them were still in their initial "trial membership" of either 7 or 30 days, and another 12 had been comped a membership and agreed to upgrade once their comp ended.

That means, at the time of my "bestseller" status, I only had about 80 people who had given me any money at all.

Of those, another 17 people were on "hardship scholarships", where they pay as little as $1/yr for their membership.

The day I got the email of my bestseller status, my gross annualized revenue was $4,211. That's 83% of the expected $5,050 that a $50/yr membership should generate over the course of a year for 101 members.

Of course, the calculation of your gross annualized revenue is completely bonkers as a metric in the first place.

Gross annualized revenue: This is how much money you make per year before Substack's fees and credit card transaction fees (charged by Stripe). This figure is annualized, meaning that we look at your revenue at any given time and figure out what it would look like over the course of 12 months, assuming the mix of monthly and annual subscriptions remains constant. -Substack

How much money have I actually made to date, though? Substack doesn't tell me. Even though there are a bajillion metrics in my dashboard, I have to go into Stripe to find how much I've actually been paid by Substack.

Since I have a half dozen different websites hooked up to Stripe, this means I have to spend a bunch of unnecessary time trying to pin down how much Substack has actually paid me.

To find this information, I had to go to STRIP>PAYMENTS>EXPORT and export all my payments.

Then, I had to sort to find the ones that looked right. It seems like when Substack creates a payment, the description is **Subscription Creation**, and when they invoice in future months, the description is **Invoice XXXXXXXX-XXXX**.

Why is this so hard? I don't know, but when I deleted and sorted "properly", it looks like my payments added up to **$2514.30**. Perhaps they don't want you to be able to easily find out how little you've actually made for months of work, but I've never had a payment partner be this opaque with their numbers.

I should have easy access to this number right on the dashboard without having to search and guess. The nice thing about subscriptions is that they build over time. So, assuming I don't royally muck it up, I should be able to maintain and build on this number in 2024.

Still, for some context, I've run three of my own Kickstarters and been involved in three others. The ones I personally ran raised **$24,541**. The ones others ran with/for me raised **$34,591**. Together, they raised **$60,132**.

Revenue is deceptive, so here is the profit I made from each campaign after production, printing, and shipping.

- The Obsidian Spindle Saga (Books 1-8)—$3,233.54
- This is NOT a Book—$3,271.30
- The Wicked Witch Academy duology—$2,800.39
- Cthulhu is Hard to Spell paperback campaign (Books 1-3)—$2,379.40
- Ichabod Jones: Monster Hunter card game—$680.74

That's a total profit of **$12,365.97** across these five campaigns. Whether you take the total revenue of just my campaigns (***10%***), total campaign revenue (***4%***), or profit across those five campaigns (***20%***), getting a Substack bestseller tag is a fractional share (***4%-20%***) of what I earn on Kickstarter alone.

This is not to knock Substack at all. Memberships are an entirely different business model, but it does show that bestseller status is a nice feather in your cap, and it's great to strive for, but it doesn't mean you'll suddenly be making bank.

Additionally, this is only a comparison against one income source. I also co-own a conference and course business, consult with authors, and work with book marketing clients that have generated substantially more than what I showed above. I can't share with you all my total revenue since Writer MBA does not have a full transparency policy, but this is how much revenue I have generated going back to 2016 that I can share.

Please note that this breakdown includes my mortgage and my salary, so this year is not quite as bad as it looks from the expenses. Total cash-on-hand and investments are up ***13.06%*** from last year, and last year was a record year for us. So, we're doing just fine at the moment.

From this, you can see how much revenue I generate every year compared to how much money it takes to become a Substack bestseller.

That said, I am only charging $5/mo or $50/yr. If I raised my price, then my revenue would likely increase.

Additionally, I have to state again in no uncertain terms that this is not a knock on Substack. Memberships tend to grow much slower than other areas of your business, and I'm happy that one is finally working for me after years of struggle. I only reveal all these numbers to show that a Substack bestseller doesn't mean that much financially in and of itself.

It definitely means something, though. It means over 100 people have committed to going on a journey with you, and that's amazing.

Now that I've beaten the financial dead horse, let's talk strategy. I've been thinking a lot about how to break this down, and I think the only way it will make sense is chronologically.

The beginning

I started my Substack journey on August 12th, 2021, after a few of my comic book friends convinced me they were getting organic reach here, and I decided to see for myself. I wasn't in the headspace to create a full publication, but I got five subscribers that first day.

I then proceeded to do nothing with it until February 8th, 2023. In the intervening two years, I was able to accumulate 31 subscribers, doing literally nothing.

On February 11th, Monica and I decided to start sharing both of our Substacks with our audiences. Monica had already been putting effort into her Substack, *The Author Analyst*, for a while, but I wasn't quite ready to dive into Substack with both feet. The day after we shared my publication, it leaped from 31 to 52 subscribers.

Then, I didn't do very much until March 13th, when Facebook vanished me. Here's what I said about it then:

Last Monday, after Facebook flagged my ad account for no reason, they signed me out of mobile, preventing me from using their code generator to sign into my account using the 2-factor authentication on their app.

I have no access to my pages or anything.

There is literally no way to get Facebook live support anymore, and they caught me in a bizarre loop that prevents me from getting a code, and the only way to get the code is to sign into Facebook where they have the code.

It's the kind of Sisyphusian feedback loop that would make the vengeful gods of old proud.

As such, I was locked out of my account, effectively hacked by the company that owns all the interactions I've built up for nearly 15 years.

Worse than locking me out, they then deleted my account, along with tens of thousands of interactions, comments, posts, etc., from my entire history on Facebook.

Locking my account pissed me off, but deleting everything I have ever posted is a bridge too far. I was once the staunchest defender of Facebook, but now I realize that I was nothing to them.

They have literally proven that in an instant.

Luckily, we were prepared for this eventuality. This email list gives me the power to reach out to you even though I no longer have a social media presence. Our Circle community, Slack, and other apps allow me to still work with partners and students.

For instance, I started this Substack a while ago and was already cross-posting between here and on Facebook.

What's nice about Substack is that it functions a lot like a decentralized social platform. I have access to the emails of all my subscribers, but I can follow along on the app and scroll through feeds like on Facebook.

Being prepared with backups and enough redundancy that I was beginning to think I was paranoid has its advantages. I have already backed up every post I've ever made for the past seven years, which I always thought was a bit bonkers, but now I realize it was both prudent and prescient.

I preach about it all the time, but in this instance, I am the living embodiment of everything I have warned about for years. If you wondered if I was a kook or not to constantly scream to the hills about owning your data, this should be your answer...

...It is very convenient to be on Facebook. I know I said that to myself a million times over the years. However, they own the data, and they can do whatever they want with it. If they see fit to take it all away from you, they will do it, and there's nothing you can do about it.

All you can do is create an ecosystem where you have access to the people that matter to you, your network of creators, your fans, your friends and your family, and make sure it can't be taken away from you.

Between February 11th and March 13th, I had gone from 31 to 65 subscribers.

I nearly doubled my subscribers in the subsequent month, but it would be lying to say I was giving even minimal effort. That all changed when Facebook vanished me. I had been working with Circle for a while, but it hadn't really been going well. I decided that if I wanted to own the customer relationship, I needed a change. This was the moment when I decided to go all in on Substack.

Going paid

Backing up just a bit to that February 11th date, when Monica and I decided to start telling our audience about Substack, I also decided to "go paid". I got my first paid subscriber on the first day.

By March 14th, I had four paid subscribers.

I consider this the nadir point when I started to focus on growth and designing a publication to attract new readers. Until now, most of the information I posted on Substack was reposted from Facebook.

Substack has a lot of guidance on going paid. I didn't listen to any of it. One day, I just decided it was time to focus on Substack, and I turned on paid. I didn't attract a lot of people at first, but enough that it showed there was a little bit of traction there.

I wrote an article about going paid. It's all worth a read, but this is an exercise I think is hugely valuable and might help you.

The easiest way to convince yourself that paid subscribers are getting value from their membership is to take out a piece of paper and create a value stack where your paid subscribers get at least a 10x return for their investment.

Most Substacks that I see have a $5/mo or $50/yr membership tier. I think we can all agree that if somebody will get $500 in value from a $50 investment, then that's a pretty amazing deal.

If you plan on a $50/yr membership, then you need to find a way to provide $500/yr of value to somebody who joins.

This might sound like an insurmountable amount, but when you break it down, value is everywhere.

For instance, let's say you have a blog about making awesome salads, and your value is providing easy-to-prepare healthy salads that taste great. I will literally share every salad post I find with my wife because we are always looking for good salads. Even in Los Angeles, we have a heck of a time finding great ones.

If you have this kind of blog, then how many hours are you saving the average person who now doesn't have to scour the internet looking for healthy alternatives every week? Colloquially, I would say that we spend at least one hour a week looking at recipes.

The median salary for a worker in the USA is $54,132, which is an hourly rate of around $27/hr. So, if your stated goal was to save paid subscribers at least 1 hour a week, that's a value of $1,404 right there over a year.

Then, can you provide a checklist, cheat sheets, a short audio/video/email course with best practices, compilation books of your best posts, or something you can create once and give people at launch? Or could you provide a meal planning guide to save even more time?

When people go paid on my Substack, they get access to several courses relevant to my audience's interests, including ***How to Build an Audience from Scratch, Write a Great Novel, 10x your Productivity***, and the archives from my long-running podcast ***The Complete Creative***, which I pulled down from everywhere in 2020, even if you only sign up for a 7-day free trial.

With Sparkle;

If you want to make 'bestseller', you have to think hard about your network. You then have to get your network to your publication and either make the deal so good they want to sign up or use special offer coupons toward your 101 count. The best seller badge is brilliant social proof, so once you get there and are committed to serving value, you'll stay there.

The first design (and redesign)

Originally, I decided to call my publication *The Author Ecosystem*, based on a concept I had been working on for a couple of years at that point. Between March 15th and April 24th, I was building *The Author Ecosystem*.

During that same time, Monica and I were developing an archetype system, and it just happened to align perfectly with the Author Ecosystem brand. By that time, I had 15 paid subscribers and 308 total subscribers.

This meant ceding *The Author Ecosystem* to our company and completely changing the name of my publication. We had decided to do something pretty bonkers on the 28th, so I had to make some drastic changes pretty quickly.

I decided on *The Author Stack* (authorstack) because I assumed it would show up pretty prominently on a search for #authorstack. Additionally, I talk a lot about "the stack" and becoming a "full stack author". So, I thought it would fit with the stuff I already talked about in my articles.

Comping 25,000 members

When that rebrand was done on April 27th, 2023, I had 378 subscribers and 15 paid subscribers.

Then, on the 28th, I started comping my main email list. We gave everyone on our Writer MBA email list a free three-month subscription. I also gave everyone on my 20,000-person writer email list a three-month comped subscription as well.

It took until May 12th to figure out the comps and get everyone situated, and by then, I had 21 paid subscribers.

It should be noted that this strategy caused a big hit to my gross annualized revenue. As some of my paid members were on one or both of those lists, my income took a dip. On May 11th, my gross annualized revenue was **$1,060**.

At the lowest point of the dip, it went down to **$740**, even though I had more paying members than ever.

It rebounded after that, but oof. It was a big hit. ***So, why did I do it?*** I talked about that in my article about Substack sections, but here is the relevant part.

I have 20,000 people on my fiction email list and close to 5,000 on our Writer MBA list. Both those mailing lists had become hyper-focused on promotions and launches without offering that much value-based content. I wanted to change that and make more posts like these.

Except I ***was*** making them...***I was just making them here on Substack***. On top of that, I was writing specifically for the exact kind of people who were already on our mailing lists. Our best stuff is behind a paywall in our membership, but the next best is made right here.

It made complete sense to bring all of them to Substack (*I can't overstress that these were people who had already opted-in to our lists*). Once we made that decision, the question became how could I shower them with love and attention so they got excited to get more emails from me. If you haven't guessed, I'm a tundra, so ***excitement is my superpower.***

Here are some things I considered and how I thought through them.

I already had people unsubscribe from my paid Substack subscription, citing a lack of content, so I had to be hyperfocused on delivering tons of value. Because of our extensive network of courses, I was able to offer $50+ in free courses to new members from the beginning, but that still wasn't enough for some paid subscribers. So, I decided to upload almost my entire back catalog of solo nonfiction and fiction books to Substack so people could see the value immediately. My audience is made up of authors and other creators, fantasy readers, and comics fans. So, I catered our bonus content to excite each segment. I uploaded multiple fantasy novels, almost my entire comic library, and my collection of solo nonfiction books. Plus, I added some mystery and science fiction novels into the mix as well. I made sure to service all of them with something meaty that I thought would pique their interest.

Then, I strategically decided to increase my weekly output. My posts are long and complicated. They pull on many disciplines and have dozens of links. So, I couldn't commit to another one of those, but I could do a weekly round-up post of my favorite Substacks (*I read hundreds*) and serialize one of my series without much extra work. It takes me about 30 minutes to make my weekly roundup post and maybe 30 minutes to schedule out my serializations for the month, and that already tripled my output in less than an hour a week. Both my weekly wellness post and my serialized novels are in their own sections that people can unsubscribe to individually if they don't want to see those posts.

Once I had those two things in place, I needed to give subscribers a reason to check it out by paywalled content, which is why we comped everyone already on my list with a three-month paid membership. I needed them to feel like this was a big perk, not a burden, so giving them something that had tangible value made sense. ***I find that people get excited about getting more content from you and less so about getting more promotions from you.*** Substack is all value. ***Now, I have three months to***

show them that value. Can I do it? I don't know, but I have done everything I can to make it worthwhile for them. Maybe 10% of people will get excited to continue their membership, or maybe 10 will, but I feel confident that I've delivered as much value as I can to demonstrate that it's not a waste of time. Now, I just have to prove it.

More than any of the reasons above, I love experimenting with weird things nobody else would try. I'm really into first-hand data and have said for years that ***I either want to be a horrible warning or a shining example, and I don't much care which one***.

My bet was that if I could comp people for three months and let them see all the value, then they would want to stick around and pay for content. On top of all that, Substack claimed that 5-10% of your free subscribers would eventually become paying members, and ***the allure of 2,500 paid members was too much to pass up.***

*[**SPOILER ALERT:** This might be true for people who find you through the internal Substack network, but I have certainly not found it true with imported subscribers, even if they have already bought something from you on another platform.]*

One last thing I will note: if you are importing multiple different lists, then make sure there are no duplicates. I didn't do my due diligence, so ***some people were comped up to 9 months when it was all said and done***. Don't be like me, be better than me.

The slow, steady climb

After doing those imports, I decided to spend the summer providing maximum value. My content schedule includes a serialized novel chapter that is released every Monday, an article or tutorial every Wednesday, and then a weekly digest every Saturday filled with links to other articles I loved during the week. Plus, members have access to a dozen novels and all three of my nonfiction books.

Between May 12th and July 18th, I grew from 21 to 45 paid members.

Between July 28th and August 12th, over 4,000 members would lose their comped status, so I decided to prepare for it by culling anyone who hadn't opened even one email in the preceding three months. Here's what I wrote about that first purge.

I just cut almost 8,000 people from my email list, and I am freaking out a bit.

I know you're probably thinking, "I don't even have 8,000 emails", or "I would kill for that many emails, and you just threw them away".

I have agonized about it for months, but there is a good reason.

Three months ago, I comped them all 3-months, and they haven't opened even one email since then.

In fact, according to Substack's activity, they aren't even one star. They are literally zero star subs.

How did they even get on my list? Well, I added them from another mailing list that I keep in Flodesk.

I added over 25,000 people from Flodesk here, and I told myself that even if they read ONE email, I would keep them.

They read ZERO.

I know people have strong feelings about cutting people from your list, but I could have a list of 150,000 right now...but what is the use of that if nobody opens?

I guess I could go to sponsors and use it as bait, or I could at least have over 100,000 subscribers when somebody clicks...but all of that is vanity.

You want people on your list that read your work. There is no real value in keeping people who never open or who have never opened.

If you're just building from the Substack Network, you can get away with never culling your list, but when you start integrating other things, that is when you'll need to think about it...

...That's a lot, but I'm pretty excited that 17,000 of those people did engage. It was absolutely worth it to run this experiment, and I will do it again.

More importantly, I couldn't watch my open rate be artificially deflated by that much.

That's 28% of my list that I knew would never engage, which means, hopefully, my next email will have a 40-50% open rate like it did before I added this last group of people.

This is the last thing I will say: all of these "dead" emails came from a group of 9,000 people who I imported last. Before then, all the emails were still getting a huge open rate.

Looking back, I probably should have waited to cull until after the next part of my strategy, but hindsight is 20/20. ***It was surely nice to see a 10% increase in my open rate after this purge with no discernable decrease in the number of opens.***

Between July 28th and August 12th, 4,500 members lost their comp status, and my total paid subscribers only rose from 45 to 69. As members lost their comp status, some of them unsubscribed, and I purged still more until I stabilized my list on August 12th.

Between April 28th and May 12th, 2023, I comped over 25,000 of my long-term subscribers between a 3-6 month trial of *The Author Stack*.

In the last 30 days, as people have been falling off their subscriptions, I've been using that opportunity to trim my list of inactive subscribers that came from those imports.

The first time, the people I cut didn't negatively impact my opens much and significantly increased my open rate. We'll see if the same is true this time.

The next date of note is October 28th, when 10,500 people come off their free trial.

With each trial ending, several people have signed up for paid memberships, but that number is nowhere near the level I thought I would see from the trials expiring.

On April 28th, I had 17 paid. Currently, I have 68. I did launch three books during that time, which raised a combined $19,630, which likely takes away from people subscribing as a paid member.

Still, I'm happy to see so many people are still reading. I basically get close to or more than 10,000 opens every time I post something, which is a nice boost to the ego if nothing else.

At the lowest point, my subscriber count dipped to 17,960.

However, I'm still getting roughly the same number of opens as I did before culling. It might be down a couple hundred opens for every article I post, but it's within a standard margin of error of where it was with a 25,000+ person list.

The margin of error in statistics is **the degree of error in results received from random sampling surveys**. A higher margin of error in statistics indicates less likelihood of relying on the results of a survey or poll, i.e., the confidence in the results will be lower to represent a population. -QuestionPro

One time offer

If you're following along, then currently, you will note that 69 paying members on even a 17,000-person list is nowhere near the 5-10% Substack talks about in their conversion percentage discussions.

Not every writer makes six figures overnight; some of the most successful writers on Substack took months to get to where they are today. The good news about subscription businesses is that recurring revenue is more steady and predictable than selling one-off content, like a book or an article.

Even so, as you continue on your journey as an independent writer, you'll have to experiment with ways to keep growing. ***We tend to see 5-10% of free subscribers convert to paying subscriptions***, with 10% being a rate to aim for. If your conversion rate is significantly below 10%, use tried-and-true tactics from other writers to improve it. -Substack

I'm not surprised at the fact my number is currently under 1%. I expected that with the introduction of Notes and more casual readers, the actual conversion percentage would be closer to 1%.

Additionally, I assumed that the highest conversion percentage would come from people who found my publication through the Substack network, as they were already "bought-in" to the subscription model. ***This has certainly been the case.***

I had always converted roughly 1-2% of my audience into my Kickstarters, and that was what I expected here, too. I'm not surprised by the results, but I am a bit disappointed in them.

That said, I was still pretty close to the 101 paid subscribers that it took to get a checkmark next to your name.

Paying readers, not Substack, decide who gets a badge. We don't give out these badges for subjective reasons, and they can't be bought. They are assigned solely according to how many paid subscribers a writer has on

Substack. Upon qualifying for a badge, writers will receive a congratulatory email and can choose whether or not to display their badge.

The badges come in three colors:

- **Purple**: tens of thousands of paid subscribers.
- **Orange**: thousands of paid subscribers.
- **White**: hundreds of paid subscribers.

I was only 31 away on August 12th. On August 13th, I sent out a winback offer.

One of the key elements of a successful winback offer is to **provide value and urgency to your customers.** You want to show them what they are missing out on and why they should act fast. You can offer value in different ways, such as discounts, freebies, upgrades, or loyalty rewards. -Linkedin

I created a segment of subscribers who chose not to continue their subscription and sent them the following email.

SUBJECT: [ONE TIME OFFER] Pay what you can afford pricing

Hi!

Lots of you reached out after your comps ended saying that you would love to support, but you couldn't afford $50/yr for a subscription, so I thought I would meet you where you are and allow you to pay what you can afford for a very limited time.

All you have to do is click on the link below that matches your budget, and ***you'll get that discount forever****. I'm only offering this discount to a select group, and you only have until the end of the month to commit before it goes away forever.*

I can't imagine a scenario where I would offer this steep a discount to you a second time. So, if you're interested, I highly suggest you take advantage now so you don't forget and lose out.

Remember, paid members don't only get access to my article archive. They can also read over a dozen of my favorite novels and comic books, including Ichabod Jones: Monster Hunter, Anna and the Dark Place, My Father Didn't Kill Himself, and more, plus all of my solo nonfiction books.

You'll also receive access to a bundle of courses valued at $60, including Write a Great Novel, 10x Your Productivity, How to Build an Audience from Scratch, and the complete 200-episode archive of The Complete Creative.

- 0% off ($50/yr)
- 20% off ($40/yr)
- 40% off ($30/yr)
- 60% off ($20/yr)
- 80% off ($10/yr)
- 90% off ($5/yr)
- 98% off ($1/yr)

All discounts of 80% and below apply to both monthly and yearly plans. The 90% and 98% discounts are only available on a yearly basis.

This is completely on the honor system. I'm trusting you to pay what you can afford, but if you abuse the system, then that's okay, too. I would prefer it if you didn't, but all I can control is the karma I put out into the world.

Happy reading,

Russell

There are a couple of things to note about this offer. The most important of which is that every word is true. Several people did email and tell me they couldn't afford to pay full price.

The second thing is that this offer really did go away on August 31st. **I strongly believe in the pay-what-you-can-afford model**, especially for counties with pay disparity. If you email me at *russell at wannabepress dot com*, I would be happy to discuss a hardship scholarship with you.

I never want money to get between somebody reading my work. That said, it's not something that I advertise, and I do hope people use it responsibly. However, if they abuse the system, that's their karma. I don't have time to worry about somebody scamming me out of $5.

I know I give way more than $50/yr in value. Any one of these posts could easily make you $500.

By the following week, I was up to 82 paid members.

On the 23rd, I was up to 86. On the 24th, I sent a follow-up email telling everyone who didn't choose to upgrade that they only had one week left. I ended that day with 103 paid members and 7 on the free trial.

Even though I only got the email on the 25th, I saw the badge come through at 10:30 AM or so. **When I checked, I had 93 Paid and 8 Free Trials**, which is why I assume that free trials count toward the overall total.

For those of you saying, "I didn't know we can email people!" Yes, you can. All you have to do is go to DASHBOARD>SUBSCRIBERS and click on the box next to a certain subscriber's name. It will come up with a box that says EMAIL.

You can also create filters or check the box on the left of where it says Subscriber at the top to select everyone on that page. It should say something like **50 matching readers selected**. Select all XXX.

If you'd like to email everyone in that segment, click the **Select all XXX** link and then email. I really dislike it when people fill my Substack inbox with special offers. I would much rather they email me and keep my app filled with nothing but articles.

As far as I know, this bypasses the “disable email” option in the settings. So, if you email people through this method, it will get to people’s inboxes, even if they disabled emails. **This is the one downside of using it, so use it sparingly.**

One-time offer, redux

Between October 24th and November 12th, 2023, 12,110 members lost their comped status.

Therefore, since I had a successful time with it the first time, I thought I would run the same one-time offer again. It should be noted that it was impossible to segment out the people who got the offer the first time, so I actually sent this offer to 16,300 people. Since there were 2.5x the number of people losing their comped status the second time, I expected 2.5x more new members than last time.

The first time I ran this in August, I received 70 new paid subscribers. This time, it was 130. Based on the tracking I've been doing all year, I thought it was possible to hit 300 paid subs this year. I just passed that number after this second round of one-time pricing.

I've got a lot of other ways to bring in revenue, so I don't know how much you can use me as a model, but I've only seen a 1.5% conversion rate, which is again right around the 1-2% I would expect but far below the 5-10% Substack claims.

I've recently added another round of uploads to my Substack, and I have 400 people coming off their comps in January, so I might run this one more time to try and hit 500 members, but I think this is probably the last time I'm running this playbook.

The only reason I ran it this time was because so many people on my old lists have supported me for years. It's not something I want to offer people who are new to my ecosystem. It's something I wanted to give as a gift to people who have been around for a long time.

This is where I stand right now on 12/2/23, with 310 paid subscribers paying an average of $28/yr.

Before this, on November 15th, I had 180 subscribers with a gross annualized revenue of $7,271, for an average of $40/yr. As you can see, while I got more paid members, it came with a significant hit to my average subscriber revenue.

For me, it's worth it to make that sacrifice to build a more robust membership base. As I mentioned, I have several other streams of revenue that fund my business. This subscriber revenue is something I plan to build slowly over time so that it can support me in the future. I hope that by the end of 2024, I can increase my membership to 1,000 active members with over a million page views a month.

That would necessitate roughly a 300% increase in both in the next year. Since I'm focusing mainly on those two metrics, focusing on my gross annualized revenue would work in direct conflict with that goal.

Comps (finally) ending

On April 28th, 2023, I comped 25,000 subscribers from my previous mailing list to ***The Author Stack***. Because of some mistakes I made while uploading my list, some people received 9+ months of comped access, which finally ended on 1/26/24.

On December 1st, there were 310 paid subscribers, and now there are 353. That's not incredible by any stretch, and 39% of them came from the Substack network, but that's still a significant amount of money. My publication is at $10,700 in gross annualized revenue, and if $6,000 of that is from my old comp list, and I get a chance to grow my relationship with them in a non-salesy way, it was probably worth it. Due mostly to running ads, I've been able to grow my publication by over 2,000 subscribers since December 1st as well, but that doesn't help us get to 1,000 paid subscribers, so I'll leave it there.

Anniversary pledge drive

After the comps ended and settled, I thought it would be a good time to host another pay-what-you-can-afford pledge drive. I started with 362 paid members and decided to offer discounts from 0% ($50) to 80% ($10).

My gross annualized revenue was $10,831 before I did the pledge drive.

I ran it from February 1st, 2024, to February 19th, 2024. When it was over, I had 473 paid members and $12,647 in gross annualized revenue.

This will be the last time I offer $10 or $15/yr pricing, and unsurprisingly, those were the two most popular tiers. Interestingly, we were able to get as many new members at $10/$15 as we did when we offered $1/$5 tiers. We'll offer this again in May, with $20 being the lowest tier, and I'm interested to see if we can maintain this level of enrollment.

The "correction"

I thought we ended on a bonkers high when we finished our last pledge drive, but I'm surprised to see so many people fall off so quickly. I thought when I started guest posts that it would be a boon to subscriber growth, but I haven't seen that as such. I thought it would be great for retention. Honestly, it hasn't been great for either.

I have seen people stop their payments more with guest articles than my own...

...but, I want to do that stuff, and I want to center other people's stories because that makes us better writers.

Often, people look at me like a business stooge, but I only know all the rules so I can break most of them. I know what I want out of my career and what I should expect from my career so that I can chart a course that makes sense to me.

Also, ***a lot*** of people do like it. Over 10,000 people read just about any post from anyone on my publication, and it's usually over 12,000 people at least.

For many publications, that is more reads than they get in a month, and it's important for me to keep doing that work for the industry at large and for those writers specifically.

I think it's important to center other voices even if my subscribers don't, and I think over time, they will agree with me if they think about it. Are these people maybe unsubscribing to become a paid member at one of my contributor's Substack? ***Well, I hope so.***

I want to drive growth for them, even if it takes it away from me.

One of the hardest things to do in business is to force other people to take their medicine. Almost every business book I've ever read tells you to do the things your customers ***want***, but I care mostly about what they ***need.***

I have no idea which one of these posts will sing with a reader, but I know one of them will if they stick with it. Knowing how to do marketing and sales helps me do that and craft a long-term narrative about how to build a thriving, sustainable business with people who stick with it, even though most people won't.

Also, they can get what they ***want*** anywhere. They probably do, in fact, and it doesn't work. ***They don't know why it's not working, but they know it doesn't work.***

That's my job as a writer, an editor, and a curator.

Why would somebody subscribed to my publication know what they need? They don't even know how to surface their problem, let alone deal with it.

I know what they need because I've been through the shit of it and know all the pitfalls.

When you don't give people what they want, they leave, and they do...a lot, for all sorts of reasons. When you placate them, they stay, docile and happy.

They also stay complacent, and I'm not about that life.

By all metrics, this is bad business. I know what people want. I could give it to them. They would never leave. They would think they are happy...

...but they would be miserable. I don't want you to be happy. I want you to be content. I want you to thrive.

I want you to take your fucking medicine.

Even if this number drops to $0 GAR, I'm still going to do it because it's important work to do, whether it's appreciated or not.

Nobody ever revolutionized an industry by giving people what they want or even what they need.

They did so by giving them something they didn't even know they wanted or needed in a way that suddenly made it all make sense for them!

There are plenty of people who will feed you convenient lies and false platitudes. Their bank account will always be fatter than mine because I deal in harsh truths.

***

With Sparkle—I love Russell's adventures in going paid. My biggest success in conversion was offering people two weeks of free access to my membership over the Christmas holidays. I do the odd experiment to see if I can drive up paid, but for the most part, I accept I have two types of people who pay—the monthlies who want to have a look around and grab some takeaways, and the annuals who want to give themselves time to build a world-class Substack. I also use the founding member tier to host what I call 'My Diamond Members', and honestly, those guys get all my gold plus guest expert workshops. I also focus on a ton of community building and collaboration between my members.

***

How to get noticed on Substack

Subscriptions are probably the hardest business model, at least to get going, and a lot of the advice is basically, "It's really hard for a long time, and then it all takes off at once".

While you're on the "really hard" part of the growth curve, it's...really hard.

The only thing you want to know is, "When will it start getting easier, bro"?

Unfortunately, the only advice somebody can give is, "IDK, maybe never", because nobody knows anything.

That's not a cynical stance, either. I've worked in publishing for most of my adult life and in creative fields since I graduated college.

The best we have come up with is:

When something is a hit, ride it hard and hope people don't eventually lose interest and turn your hit into a money pit.

Make a lot of bets on many different projects and hope that one takes off.

I'm (Russell) not kidding. One of those two is the business model of every creative business that exists.

Either they found a hit and are riding it, they are putting out a bunch of quality products and betting on the law of averages, or they are doing both.

When you're building a subscription business, putting pennies in the bank, like Monica says, it's really hard to do either of those things. You're basically banking on one thing before it is a hit and hoping it takes off. The economics of creativity don't often work in your favor.

On top of that, there are celebrities, top-tier journalists, world-class reporters, editors from the biggest magazines on Earth, bestselling authors, and more.

How can you even get anyone to notice little ol' you?

Well, I built a career without any of that stuff and currently have a publication with 15,000+ subscribers, so there is hope, even if it doesn't seem that way.

It's tough. I won't lie to you, but it's also possible if you have the right tools.

First, the elephant in the room. Yes, I have an audience now. Yes, I'm a *USA Today* bestselling author. Yes, I've been a six-figure author since 2017.

That's me now, but I built that all from being a nobody. When I started, I had a comic nobody wanted and a dream.

That I was able to do it maybe means something.

On top of that, I often feel inadequate looking at all the other amazing names on this platform. While I've done some things, I'm not the editor-in-chief of *Elle*, I've never interviewed Obama, and I've never sold out Madison Square Garden.

People ask all the time why my posts are so long, and I try to explain that while most people who reach my publication know they have a problem, they have no idea the scope or depth of what they are trying to solve, so I have to show them.

Writing programs don't talk about business, and most authors don't seek out business teachers, so all they know when they come to me is that what they are doing isn't working and that they want to become successful authors.

I take the time in my posts to say, "Oh, you want to build an audience. Well, to do that, we have to break down x, y, z, and I have to teach you a, b, and c".

But in reality, it's probably because I feel inadequate. I figure if I write enough, I can justify my existence, and it will prove that I deserve to be here. So, here I go again.

The secret to success in any field

While the two bullet points at the top of this chapter are true, we can break them down further into something more usable for our purposes.

Are you ready? Here's what it takes to have success in ***any*** field or ***any*** platform for ***any*** business.

- Make something.
- Spend time building a community.
- Share your work with a ton of people in the right communities. Build friendships with people, not just surface-level platitudes. Help them grow and let them help you grow so you ***both*** get to the next level and improve together.
- Make your work even better.
- Expand your reach into new communities and increase the impact in the communities you're already in. The deeper your connection with the people in your network is, the more they will want to bat for you. The goal, eventually, is to build your own community where ***you*** are the nexus point.
- Share your new work with a ton of people. If it's better, it will resonate ***more,*** and you'll be able to gain more excitement for it. The more your work resonates, the easier it will spread through communities.

- Repeat as many times as necessary, iterating along the way, making better work, building your network, and sharing your work until you break through to the next level.

This isn't a step-by-step system. Notice I didn't number anything. They are all things you need to be doing in tandem with each other all the time from the jump in perpetuity.

You can share your work by personally reaching out, joining groups, and forming collaborations, which is marketing...

...or you can do it through running ad campaigns, which is advertising, though I would probably hold off advertising until you have something that resonates with people deeply and has built a powerful network.

How you share your work might vary slightly between industries, but the underlying process is the same: make good work, network with people, grow your network, promote their work, make it easy for them to promote your work, find more people, and repeat.

Podcasts, courses, comics, movies, television, novels; literally everything I've ever done works on the exact same underlying process.

Conventions, Amazon, Kickstarter, Substack, your own website...anywhere you want to grow your business, it's the same process.

If you aren't gaining traction, then make better stuff, change the market for your work, network more, or share your work more, either through marketing or advertising.

How you make something great, what communities you join, who you bring into your network, and how you iterate are very personal, but they should be the foundational parts of any plan you make.

The (relatively) simple math of it all

According to Substack, there are over 20 million monthly active subscribers, which means if even a fractional share could be part of your niche audience, let's say it's 1%, then that's 200,000 potential readers on the platform who are somewhat gettable. Obviously, some niches will be smaller, and others will be much larger than that, but let's use 1% for this example.

It's imminently easier to get a subscriber who is already on Substack to become a subscriber to your publication than to get somebody to join Substack for the first time. So, the main crux of this section will be about getting noticed on Substack by subscribers already on Substack.

On top of monthly active subscribers, there are 2 million paying members on the platform. This means roughly $2/20^{th}$, or 10% of active subscribers, pay for one or more publications. Given that, if you could attract 2,000 of those already active subscribers, you would likely be able to turn roughly 200 of them into paid subscribers over time.

If you want to scale beyond that, you would need to do some simple algebra: 10X = Y, wherein X is the number of paid members you want, and Y is the total number of free subscribers you need to attract.

If you want to be conservative, you can use a 5% conversion rate. Then, the formula would be 20X = Y, or the ultra-conservative 1% would be 100X = Y. If you aren't at least getting a 1% conversion rate, you probably need to redesign your publication and tighten your message. The tighter your publication and stronger the voice, the more your conversion rate will increase.

That is still a huge task, but it feels doable. Now, we have to get them to notice and resonate with you.

How do we do that? Let's dig into it.

Your publication has to look as good as anything out there

The number one thing that every writer on Substack can do better is graphic design. So many publications look bad, especially in the cover imagery. Substack gives you free access to thousands of images and an AI image generator, so there is very little excuse for having less than top-tier graphics.

The reason I got traction in publishing was because I cared about my books looking as good as anything the Big 5 publishers put out.

All books that succeed have a base layer of quality to them where people can say, "Yup, that's a book, and it looks like it won't fall apart on me. The author looks like they can complete a story".

If you don't have that, people won't buy your book. Just because you have that doesn't mean they will buy it, of course, but if you don't have that, they almost certainly won't give you a chance to earn their attention.

Even if they will buy either way, your job as a creator who wants to grow is to remove as many points where people can say no as possible. Any time somebody is given the choice to turn away, they likely will. We call this friction.

I like to say books can be "objectively good" and "subjectively not your jam". They are two different metrics. Same with Substack. If somebody can't look at your publication and believe it is objectively good, then they will never stick around to decide if it is subjectively their jam.

Objective goodness is a metric that is the same across all books. Whether the cover is pleasing, if it reads well without a lot of errors, if the binding is sturdy, if it conforms to the format of a book, etc. We all know what a book should look like when we pick it up, and if a book doesn't look like that, we are less inclined to try it out because it doesn't mean the base level of professionalism we expect.

The same is true with publications. Think about it this way. Every beat writer has their own voice, but every newspaper has roughly the same metrics to measure objective goodness. That said, while I believe all my books reach an objective level of goodness, readers subjectively prefer some over others, and it usually vastly differs from my preferences. In fact, my best books usually never sell.

You need an ethos

There are all sorts of posts showing you how to make a great About page and create slick branding, but none of that matters if you don't have an ethos.

An ethos is not what kinds of things you're going to talk about inside your publication. It's about what transformation you are giving the reader.

Every publication I pay for not only has great writing but a unique style that delivers on the promise to the reader every time they post. They don't do this the same way every time, but they know their reader, where they are, and where they want to take them. In fact, part of what makes them great is that they keep finding new ways to bring you into the conversation. If you have an ethos, then you can talk about just about anything. After you figure it out, take that ethos and build your messaging around it. To build one, I recommend *The Official Universal Fantasy™ Substack.*

Your ethos is the brand you are creating. I know lots of writers hear the word brand and run the other way. Many talk about how branding isn't important because we each have a unique voice.

But by making that case against branding, they are actually making the case for branding because that unique voice is your brand. The whole of a brand is a distillation of how the people who resonate with your message will find you. A brand is what speaks for you when you can't speak for yourself, amplifying your message so it can be found by the people who need to hear it.

You already have a brand. It already exists inside of you, and the outward expression of that inner truth is what resonates with people.

There are millions of flashy logos and interesting-looking websites floating around the internet, but they are almost always hollow and unmemorable. I want to love them, but they leave me asking the same two questions: "What are you trying to say here?" and "Who are you trying to say it to?".

These are the two basic questions you must ask when building a brand, and too often, they are skipped over in favor of a flashy logo that screams nothing into the void but "Look at me, I'm pretty!".

This is antithetical to a brand's purpose. The purpose of a brand is to stand above the void and scream, "Look at me. I'm perfect for you!" It may be fun to have a cool logo, but flashy design doesn't serve the purpose of building a brand identity.

The purpose of a brand is to speak for you when you aren't there to speak for yourself. It's a reflection of you in the eyes of your ideal customers. Its job is to provide a beacon for your audience in the endless, hyper-connected fog in which we live.

Look at a company like Apple. Steve Jobs couldn't speak to every human being on the planet. He was a busy guy. Even if he could, he wouldn't be able to reach out again and again over the course of decades. He needed something that could repeatedly speak for him in the minds of the populace. Enter the Apple brand, which is possibly the greatest brand in the history of the world.

In Apple's advertising, logo, and design aesthetic, Jobs had to convey exactly what people could expect from his products without saying a single word to them. He had to create a brand so powerful that his perfect audience would rise from the endless void and hone in on his company.

This is what the right brand can do for your company. It can turn your audience building inside out and lead the right people to your door.

If you do it correctly, of course.

Generally, creatives go about building a brand too early in their company's life cycle. I know it's tough to hold off on branding since we have artistic energy brimming from every orifice, but a memorable brand isn't about artistic talent.

It's about the emotional connection with your audience.

Look at the "Life is Good" logo. There's almost no artistic talent needed to draw that stick figure, and yet it resonated with people so deeply they were able to build a company that's held up for decades.

The interesting thing about branding is that if you want to go slow and grow organically, the best thing you can do is spend a few hours solidifying your brand.

Why?

Because your brand speaks for you when you can't speak for yourself. It magnifies your message to cut through the noise and find your people.

It's something you can do one time that pays off for years.

I spent some time back in 2015 creating our mascot, Melissa the Wannabe, for Wannabe Press, and it has paid off for years. People identify themselves with Melissa, and I know they are my people.

I have not had to think about my publishing company's brand since 2015. Whenever I need something, I just pull that file and use it.

When I need a profile pic, I pull the pic I'm using now and just change the background color. It was made by the same artist who drew our mascot, so I know it's in alignment with everything else I do.

I probably need one without glasses or maybe with red lenses since I use migraine glasses at almost all times now.

It makes things so much easier because I know what fits in my brand and what doesn't almost immediately. I have saved countless hours worrying about what I should do by having a solid brand.

Meanwhile, I've run tons of sales, tabled at a boatload of shows, and spent thousands of hours on the rest of my marketing, but my brand has not taken even an hour of my time since then, and it has netted me countless new fans.

When I created this Substack, I spent a couple of hours finding a logo and putting everything together, and I've not had to think about it since launching *The Author Stack*.

My brand brings me new readers every day without me doing anything.

It's a significant time investment upfront, but it's the kind of work whose positive impact compounds over time.

If you want to go fast, you absolutely must get your brand right, but if you want to go slow, then the single best-leveraged thing you can do is get your brand right.

It is the foundation by which people will find you and decide whether they resonate with your work. Readers make decisions in a fraction of a second, and if you don't catch them, you might have lost them forever.

You don't have to have a slick, hip brand, either.

I talked to somebody recently who was developing a cottage-core brand where people feel safe and warm just hanging out. The brand is what speaks to your ideal reader.

You absolutely do not have to do anything with your brand or even think about marketing. I'm not trying to pressure you to feel like this is something you have to do.

However, if you are interested in finding more people who resonate deeply with what you do, then solidifying your brand is something you can do once that pays off forever.

Are they not stopping, not clicking, or not converting?

There are three big issues you need to deal with before you start getting noticed. Each of these points will make people turn away from your publication. Basically, you need to figure out if people are not stopping their scroll to check you out, if they are not clicking to read more once they stop, or if they are not converting into subscribers.

If they aren't stopping, then you have a design problem. It means your imagery/text is not exciting enough to make the reader stop scrolling. This is the hardest part of the equation, honestly.

If they aren't clicking, it means you have a messaging problem. Perhaps you have a great image, but the headline isn't something your audience cares about, bores them, or something else in the messaging is preventing somebody from clicking.

If they aren't converting, then it means you are targeting the wrong people, or your text isn't crisp enough to get them excited. It could also be that you don't have enough places to join your email list throughout your article. Also, don't design every article for the same person but the same kind of person. Everyone is going to find you at different places in their journey. You are technically the same person at every age, but you are very different, too. So, is your reader.

Once you fix those problems, you will reliably be able to get people into your publication. It's not really worth it to start scaling before you can fix these three problems. I know it's not about Substack, but it will help you picture the design elements of a page that may be holding people back from diving into your publication.

Once you have a banger publication that looks great, then it's really about being noticed.

Before this point, your efforts likely won't bear much fruit. Now that you have the rest of your publication on fleek, you should start getting people you meet excited to join your community.

If you aren't getting people excited, it means you haven't fixed the other problems yet. The biggest mistake that people make is trying to network with the biggest names in their niche. While that does surprisingly well on Substack, the people who are going to be most invested in your career are people at your level who are trying to figure it out. They are the ones you should push the hardest because they will push you the hardest.

When they grow, you grow. All of you win when you win together. This is why when you see successful people, many of the people in their network knew them before they were successful, and they all seem to have become successful together.

What is your niche?

If you don't know your niche, that's a problem. Knowing your niche is a huge part of getting noticed. There are about a hundred ways to be a humor writer, a business writer, or a tech writer. The more focused you can be, the more the right readers will resonate with you. This is especially true when you find your voice.

Once you know your niche and your voice, then it's about becoming a good steward of your niche's ecosystem and finding out how you fit into it in a healthy way. Here are some questions to ask yourself when trying to become known in your particular niche.

- Have you found all the publications in your niche?
- Are you following and subscribing to them?
- Are you communicating with them regularly?
- Do you hang out with them on Notes?
- Are you sharing their work and engaging in a positive manner?
- Do you have a unique perspective that enhances the overall conversation?

I think of the *Fictionistas* who all banded together to build a fiction community on Substack. But, even if there isn't an official community, there are still people who create the neural network of your niche. Once you find one, they are probably recommending at least one other on their page. If you already have a banger publication and know how to fit into their ecosystem, then simply plugging into the existing ecosystem will start to amplify your work.

Here's how that works in practice.

I built my name by showing authors how to use Kickstarter to build their author businesses. I had been talking about direct sales for a long time but found a way to get noticed because I was successful on Kickstarter, and authors turned to me when they wanted to learn about the platform. This allowed me to grow my own brand because I found a way to fit inside the author services ecosystem in a unique way. The ecosystem already existed for years, but I didn't grow significantly until I was able to carve out my little niche inside of it in a healthy way.

Writers at Work with Sarah Fay is focused on Substack growth, and we all know that if we have questions about Substack, she's a great resource. I constantly see her referenced. A long time ago, a producer told me it's better to be in the top 3 on a list of genre writers than be number 10 on five lists because nobody calls the tenth person.

Start being of service

What does it mean to be "of service"?

Lots of people talk about being of service to their community, but they miss one crucial point. You can't serve people if you expect anything from them. I see so many people seeking to serve to get more followers, make more money, or boost their egos.

Those people often wonder loudly why they don't get anywhere...and it almost always flows back to the fact that you expect them to buy. That is not being of service to your community. It's counterintuitive, but good things happen when you do things without expectations.

The easiest way to get results is to stop doing things expecting results and to do them to be of service. Share insights without expectation of anything in return.

I have a roundup every week filled with my favorite posts. Some of the writers I share like the post, others restack it, and still others comment, and I appreciate that, but 95% don't do/say anything, and that's fine.

I am doing it because I want people to read great Substacks and get more involved. I'm doing it to be a good steward of the ecosystem. It turns out that when you do that, good things happen.

Even though they don't all engage, I have still met a ton of amazing creators because I shared their stuff with my audience so other people could find them. If you only find one awesome connection a week, then by the end of one year, you'll have over 50 awesome connections.

I'm very strategic in only sharing things I think my audience will love. I am very protective of my audience, but I also want them to find things to love about a platform I love. When you help others win, you win.

Have you ever heard of the Goodwill Bank? It's one of my favorite metaphors, especially when people feel icky about sharing their own work.

You are going to ask for a lot from your audience when launching a product. They will be bombarded by it on every social media channel imaginable; you will be disseminating information dozens of times a day on multiple outlets. God help the people who follow you on multiple channels. They're the real heroes.

With so many updates about your product, it's easy for people to become annoyed with you and tired of your product. They will want to unsubscribe from your newsletter and unfollow you on social media. By the time your launch is over, they won't want to hear from you ever again.

The only way to combat this is to have a great relationship with your audience before you launch your product because you will torch it once your launch begins.

That's why you need to make deposits into the Goodwill Bank far in advance of any product launch. This is the crux of the value-first mentality. This is the business reason why we have to provide information to our audience and grow their trust before we ask for anything in return.

Because we will ask for something in return when we launch a product, and we will ask a lot. We will ask so much that any rational person will tune us out. But emotions aren't rational. People allow those they like and trust to get away with irrational things, like pounding them with reasons to buy their product.

That's why we need to build up massive goodwill before we even consider launching our product.

Think about your goodwill like it's a bank. We'll call it The First Bank of Goodwill. This bank works like any other bank, except that it runs on your goodwill instead of money.

When you do something nice for somebody, you make a deposit into this bank. Whether it's writing a blog post, speaking on a panel, providing advice over coffee, or even just retweeting an interesting article, everything you do for your audience is a deposit in the Goodwill Bank.

By contrast, everything you ask of your audience is a withdrawal from the Goodwill Bank. Every time you ask somebody to buy your product, every time you pitch them something, and every single time you ask them to share your posts, you are withdrawing from your goodwill account.

If you have been depositing into the Goodwill Bank over and over again, you can make these withdrawals without over-drafting your account; however, if you haven't been making these deposits, then you can't afford to make an ask of your audience. Imagine trying to buy a $50,000 boat in cash when your checking account only has $3.27 in it. You just can't do that.

The same is true with your goodwill.

If you keep withdrawing from the Goodwill Bank without making deposits, there will be nothing left in your account when you need it. Without enough goodwill, your product launch won't be successful because your audience has no reason to support you. If you keep making those deposits, then you will always have enough goodwill in your account to sustain your withdrawals.

This is where most people screw up when it comes to launching a product. They haven't spent enough time making deposits into the Goodwill Bank to sustain their withdrawals, so their ask comes across as begging. It's perceived as brash and creates an uncomfortable situation. Instead of people gladly buying the product, they either bristle at the thought of buying or only buy out of pity. This type of customer doesn't stick around for the long haul.

This is why making deposits into the Goodwill Bank is such an important concept. If you do it correctly, you'll always have a massive amount of goodwill available when it's time to launch your product. With that goodwill built up, your audience will gladly buy from you instead of recoiling from your ask.

Just note that making deposits into the Goodwill Bank is a perpetual task you must perform throughout your career. You can't just use it on your first launch and coast on the interest forever. Your goodwill account is like a checking account—it doesn't build interest.

Luckily, goodwill is easy to deposit if you are a good person who wants to serve your audience. If you come from a place of service and value, then almost everything you do will make a deposit into the Goodwill Bank.

Basically, if you think of goodwill as currency, then you have to deposit more often than you withdraw, or you will go into a deficit and overdraw.

If you do that too often, your audience will get mad and turn away.

But, if you keep depositing more often than you withdraw, then you can basically keep withdrawing as much as you want.

You have to keep a positive balance.

Find ways outside of Substack to grow

Writers on Substack seem exclusively interested in how to grow through Substack network effects, but this is myopic thinking.

I get where it's coming from. When you think about other social platforms, growth must happen exclusively on that platform.

Substack isn't like that.

In fact, almost all my growth comes from off-platform actions. Looking for subscribers off-platform contradicts what I said above. Still, the simple fact is there are billions more readers off Substack than on it, and bringing them into the Substack ecosystem is often a really good way to grow. However, you'll have a much harder time converting those subscribers into paid members because they have not necessarily bought into the paid subscription model like people already using the platform.

My growth comes from many different avenues. Mainly, it comes from BookFunnel promotions, from my Action Fantasy Book Club, from lead magnets with Writer MBA, and from conventions. Because you can upload an email list to Substack, you can grow elsewhere and import that list into your existing publication. It completely changes the dynamics when you start to look outside Substack's internal network to help fuel your growth.

The core of my business is the Good Human Strategy that undergirds my whole life. If you can get it right, a whole lot of this other stuff falls into place. It's worked for me pretty well, but I will admit it takes much longer to work than the fear-based strategies so prevalent nowadays.

There is nothing more compelling than fear when it comes to selling things. However, personally, I don't like selling on fear. It doesn't make me feel good, and while I might leave a lot of money on the table, I have no problem sleeping at night.

So, here is the strategy I use broken down into three steps.

Put good into the world with no expectation of return.

Do good work that is objectively of high quality, even if it is subjectively not somebody's cup of tea.

Show your work to as many people as possible and collect the people who resonate with it like a dragon hoarding riches.

It sounds simple, but it's taken me surprisingly far. There are tips, tricks, and hacks I will share to get the most out of this strategy, but this is the core of it all.

One of the most important things I ever learned while building my career was called The Attractive Character. It is the idea that if you become the kind of person your audience can't resist, then you will magnetize the right people to your message while repelling the wrong people.

This single concept changed a lot for me. In fact, it turned my marketing around completely. Instead of pushing my message out to everybody endlessly, I planted my flag into the ground and pulled the right people to me.

This idea is the basis for The Good Human Strategy.

In it, you start by putting good into the world and acting like a good human. Hopefully, you are already a good human, but even if you only act as a good human, you will eventually become that kind of human. It is very important that you are, at the very least, helpful and kind because those are two qualities people respond to, especially if you are helpful and kind to them.

These qualities do not work as well as fear when it comes to building loyalty quickly, but they do create a better class of fans who are loyal because they want to be loyal instead of loyal because they fear not being near you.

The most important part of this whole process is that you put good into the world without expecting anything in return. What you do is your karma and the only thing you can control. What other people do is their karma, and that's on them to handle. The world will beat you down in every way possible, but if you can find a way to put good into the world even when everything is going against you, then you win in the end.

Once you are a good human who puts good into the world for the right reasons, you must also make sure to do good work. This is the type of work that people respond to and like. If you make garbage, then people won't like it, and this strategy falls apart. Everybody doesn't have to like your work, but your work needs to resonate deeply with at least some people.

After you make good work and do good things, then you plant yourself in as many places as possible where your ideal audience hangs out, like a magnet, and allow them to find you. Once you implement the first two parts of this strategy, the rest of your life becomes about planting yourself in as many of the right places as possible, spreading your message to the right people, and waiting for them to find you.

Planting is a bit like playing music on a busy street corner. Most people walking past won't pay you any mind, but some of them will stop. If you're good enough, they'll turn around and engage with you. If you are magnetic enough, you'll start to gather a nice little crowd for yourself before too long. Does everybody who plays on the street gather a crowd? No, because most people aren't good enough or magnetic enough to sway an audience.

It's the opposite of standing on that same street corner and running around begging people to listen to your CD. This happens a lot in Los Angeles. Every time you walk up a busy street, you see one singer or another stopping people at random and begging them to give them a minute of their time.

In that scenario, you are doing the chasing. You are tiring yourself out, engaging with the wrong people, and wasting a lot of time. On top of that, you're pissing a lot of people off who just want to go about their day.

It's the same crowd you're engaging with during both scenarios, but you're engaging in a much different way. In one scenario, you run around chasing them. In the other, they come to you. It's the same crowd but with much different results. The problem becomes that when you plant, you better have something worthy of attention.

Another great way to plant is to say, "Here is my Substack!" and let the right people find you. Unfortunately, it is hard to plant without an audience already, at least with your own group, because nobody knows you...yet. This is why you need to plant in other places first, but you can direct them to where you are growing your audience, like your Substack.

Sometimes, you have to plant several times in the same place, but you can never stop planting. This is the opposite of chasing after people. It is the opposite of hustle. You are choosing where to plant, and you know what resonates with your audience. Once you have that, the right people will magnetize toward you instead of the other way around.

There are all sorts of marketing and sales strategies you need to understand to know where to plant, how to message yourself, and how to turn a casual observer into a lifelong fan, but The Good Human Strategy is simple and effective. Instead of chasing after people, become the person they need you to be, and then they will come to you.

Your career is an ecosystem. It does not exist on any one platform. It is a living, breathing thing that changes all the time. It evolves, stalls, sputters, and veers off track. You have to guide it, just as if it were a child.

The thing people always get wrong is focusing on any one platform as the only source of their success.

Yes, it's important to grow with intention, but no career is ever made on one platform. Instead, they all act like entry nodes, or spokes on a flywheel, that allow people to enter and exit.

The stronger the central hub of your flywheel is, the more your career will flourish. Yes, the spokes are important, but they are nothing without the hub.

The hub is you, your company, your series, or whatever you want to develop your brand around, but Substack, Kickstarter, Facebook, TikTok, or whichever platform is hot right now is just one spoke on the flywheel of your career.

The mistake people make is that they spend so much time reinforcing the spokes of the flywheel that the central hub crumbles into dust.

Kickstarter is a main spoke in my flywheel. Most people who come into my ecosystem monetize through Kickstarter.

It is not my only spoke, though...not by a long shot. It is also not my central hub. My central hub is about bringing people deeper into my orbit and then providing them with opportunities to spend money that makes sense to them.

The reason my career continues to thrive is that many spokes combine to reinforce each other and, most importantly, the central hub. Additionally, it means if any one platform crumbles to dust, I can detach that spoke and continue to succeed without it.

Historically, no less than 25% of my newsletter growth has come from conventions. I went to San Diego Comic-Con a few weeks ago and came back with over 1,000 new subscribers for my publication. I've talked to several Substacks that grow from Facebook ads, TikTok ads, Sparkloop, etc.

You have to expand your thinking if you're going to have exponential growth. It probably won't come from Substack alone.

However, if you have several ways to grow, then you can combine them in powerful ways.

Don't be afraid to cull

When you start to grow like this, you'll attract a lot of casual readers who don't really care about your work and fall off reading pretty quickly.

This is the only time I think it's appropriate to cull your list to make sure your deliverability is high. If you're not in a high growth trajectory, you probably don't need to cull your list. I generally try to grow pretty quickly. As such, I recently cut almost 8,000 people from my email list.

I know you're probably thinking, "I don't even have 8,000 emails", or "I would kill for that many emails, and you just threw them away".

I have agonized about it for months, but there is a good reason. These were the same ones I had comped months before and they hadn't opened anything. In fact, according to Substack's activity, they aren't even one star. They are literally zero star subscribers.

How did they even get on my list? Well, I added them from another mailing list that I keep in Flodesk.

I added over 25,000 people from Flodesk here, and I told myself that even if they read ONE email, then I would keep them.

They read ZERO.

I know people have strong feelings about cutting people from your list, but I could have a list of 150,000 right now...but what is the use of that if nobody opens?

I guess I could go to sponsors and use it as bait, or I could at least have over 100,000 subscribers when somebody clicks...but all of that is vanity.

You want people on your list that read your work. There is no real value in keeping people who never open or who have never opened.

If you're just building exclusively from the Substack Network, you can get away with never culling your list, but when you start integrating other things, that is when you'll start to need to think about it.

Stick around

80% of this work is just gathering the will to stick around another day and keep putting out great work. Yes, you get credit for consistency, but not until you stick around for a while.

No, three months is not consistent. Maybe a year is consistent, but you have to keep going past that to really get credit for it.

Three years is definitely consistency, as long as you're still putting out quality content. A hundred posts definitely shows consistency as long as they're good.

Most of the work we do as writers is just outlasting other people and continuing to put out good content. I am constantly shocked at how many people find my work just because I've been able to put out high-quality work for a long time.

I've had a weekly newsletter for almost a decade now, and I can count on one hand how many weeks I've missed.

Do you know how many people have fallen down that started with me?

Almost all of them. So many people told me they couldn't keep the consistency. These are people with a bigger audience, who made a bigger splash, and who were doing great work.

This takes a while, and it's not really fair to compare you starting on Substack with somebody who already has an audience because they put in the work. You're doing the work now, but they did the work for years to get where they are today.

You didn't see them do the work, but they walked a beat, built a network, grew a fanbase, developed a voice, and cultivated a niche.

That's the work we all do.

If you're not able to get traction even though you're putting yourself out there, then you need to go back to the design of your publication. If you have a great publication, then you need to put yourself out there in a way that positions you as a healthy part of your ecosystem.

If you do all those things, then you should be getting traction. If you're not, then it's because you haven't fixed the problem, even though you think you did. You need to go back and try again.

If you don't know where to start, go to the Search tab, look at the best publications in your category, follow them all, and subscribe to all of their recommendations. Then, they will all start showing up in your inbox and on Notes. Just keep doing that until you see patterns.

It's a lot of data points, and it can get overwhelming, even for me. Whenever I get overwhelmed, I remember I'm looking ***at*** data, and I'm looking ***for*** wisdom. It's my job to take that data, collate it into information, analyze it into knowledge, and then synthesize it into wisdom that serves you on your journey.

We are told to "scale" and "get your subscribers" basically at all costs, but after helping hundreds of authors build their businesses, I have found that the #1 cause of burnout is doing things that don't serve you.

This could be writing-related (writing a genre you don't like because it's "hot") or business-related (everyone told me I have to be on TikTok, but I hate it).

It also comes from doing too much and taking on too much at any one time, but in general, it seems like burnout is primarily your body reacting viscerally to something your soul already knows...

You weren't meant to do that work.

Once again, this is not always the case. Plenty of times, burnout is caused by doubling down on the things you love, but the kind of burnout that seems to last months is at least significantly caused by doing work your soul doesn't want to do.

This is why we created the Author Ecosystems in the first place. We found there are five main types of author growth strategies, and by and large, people burn out or don't grow because they are doing the wrong ones for them.

People come to me mostly for growth strategies, but at the end of the day, if you don't have your mind right, you will burn out before you succeed. In fact, succeeding at doing things that don't resonate with you is the nightmare scenario for most authors because they are trapped by gilded handcuffs.

Most writers lack the foundational understanding of what lights them up, what kind of audience they want to serve, and how they want to engage with the world before they scale up and are then trapped in a life they hate.

Writing then becomes a burden, and they are suffocated by the one thing that caused them joy.

So, the good news is that you can succeed by doing many different things. If Substack proves nothing else, it's that you can build an audience writing about nearly anything.

I literally would never have thought reading about salads would be riveting, but Emily Nunn has me waiting on every post. Did I think I would spend time every week reading an interview with a different older person before Substack? No, but Sari Botton made it happen, and I love it.

And there are lots of other success stories like this. If you expand out beyond Substack, I know literally thousands of authors, and the most successful ones all have very different businesses from each other, even in the same niche.

The number one most important thing you need to do is get your mind right. There are several things I tell everyone who asks for advice, and it has nothing to do with money.

- You are going to suck at first, and that's just part of it. Sucking at something is the first step to being good at something.

- Failure is part of it, too. Successful people have failed more than most people have even tried.

- You deserve to take up space just for existing, and you deserve to exist. So many people think having an audience will "fix them". Success will not fix the hole inside you. You have to decouple your self-worth from your success as quickly as possible because it will not heal you. On top of that, the things you think are broken about you are the things that make you a hero. They are the things people will resonate with about your work.

- Always optimize for enjoyment. I've left millions on the table because I didn't want to do that work.

- Bet on people, not companies. Companies lay people off. They change. They morph. They become things you no longer recognize. The right people are better bets. Follow them wherever they go.

- Choose a group you want to serve. Then, serve them long enough that they overcome the feeling that you will abandon them.

- Find ways to add value: monetarily, emotionally, mentally, and physically. But don't give so much of yourself that you can't recover. People need you at your best, and that means rest is critical.

- People want to support you. Let them—however they can, whenever they can. You don't have to do it alone.

Yes, getting your money right is important, but you don't have to monetize if you aren't ready. You can keep working as a hobby forever. Writing wasn't even a viable profession until after WW2, and it's only been the last decade or so that we have had a writing class, especially one that can sustain itself outside of New York and Los Angeles.

It's okay to do this stuff for the fun of it, but even if you want to make money, you should still do this stuff for the fun of it.

There are thousands of ways you can make yourself miserable doing this work. So much of running a successful business is set up to drain your energy. If you're going to take this journey, the writing itself shouldn't be one of them. If I wanted to be miserable, I would get a job.

***

With Sparkle—I pay a VA to schedule pins to Pinterest to grow my Substack, I talk about it on my Instagram when I feel like it, and I have a YouTube playlist dedicated to joyful, sustainable growth on Substack. All of these things 'work', but the majority of my subs come through Substack. I don't run ads, so this is low cost and all pretty high reward for me. I can have a brand new subscriber dm me and ask for my 1-2-1 link, which is the highest-priced ticket thing I offer. No nurture, no sequence, no selling—they just find me and think, yep, this is the gal I need. Expert status is rated, of course, but more than anything, I think it's because I keep my message clear and repeat it often!

***

How to find more readers for your books and get stacked with subs

One of the biggest problems that writers face is how to get more readers to their work. I've (Russell) talked before about going paid on Substack, but how do you get a critical mass of readers to make going paid worth it?

I've spent my nonfiction career at the intersection of art and commerce, and one of my specialties has been mailing list growth. I've helped thousands of authors grow their mailing lists into sustainable businesses that light them up inside.

So, today, I'm going to share with you my favorite and most effective ways to build your mailing list, whether that's on Substack or somewhere else. Some of these will resonate more with you than others, and that's how it's supposed to be in the end. Hopefully, over time, you can build more and more into your routine.

Prelaunch your book or paid membership on Kickstarter/your website/Indiegogo

I am a launcher. I love focusing 100% of my attention on discrete marketing events for a fixed amount of time. I don't do well with continuous dribbles of money. I like to turn the faucet on at full blast and then turn it off again soon after.

This is also how I acquire the largest percentage of my new readers. Yes, the people who buy whatever I'm selling sign up for my list, but I also offer free previews, workshops, seminars, webinars, and other content in service of the launch, which is how I get even more emails.

These launches happen outside of retailers, where I can collect email addresses from my most loyal fans and segment my list by interest. You can do this on your own website or with direct sales platforms like ClickFunnels, but I find Kickstarter works best because there is some organic reach there, too.

Even if you don't have a "book" per se, you can still launch a paid membership by having a 2-3 week launch event with special bonuses for joining.

Or you can have a sneaky launch by putting together a collection of your best posts and articles into a collection of essays like I just did on Kickstarter.

This book wasn't originally going to exist, but when I shared the idea with people, they fell in love with it immediately.

Everything in *This is Not a Book* was written either on Facebook, my old blog, or in emails between 2015-2022. Aside from the introduction, I didn't write anything new for it, and it still made thousands of dollars.

I hired an editor and used Book Cover Zone to find a cover, plus DepositPhotos to find a nice chapter header image. It cost about five hundred dollars to put the book together. I was absolutely floored by how many people wanted a totem of my best work collected into one place, even though every word had previously been given away for free.

I had already tried this several years ago with my book *How to Become a Successful Author*, but it was not nearly as successful because I didn't put focused attention on it through a launch event. Instead, I just put it on retailers, and it did fine, but not nearly as well as the Kickstarter. Plus, I didn't get those subscribers, which is key for long-term growth.

If you look at the campaign, you'll see that backers could get a 1-year Substack membership for $75+, but even if you didn't buy it, you effectively helped fund the newsletter by supporting the book. Additionally, dozens more people signed up to get a free preview of the book.

Maybe people don't want to buy a subscription because it is a continuous commitment, but they are often happy to buy a book that you have curated, even if it is close to the same price as a membership.

Even though I've run 30+ campaigns, roughly 1/3 of my buyers are new to me, and 80% of them sign up for my mailing list once the campaign is done.

Just be careful. You can't just add people to your mailing list if they buy your book. You have to ask them if they would like to join in the post-campaign survey, and most people do.

If you want to learn more about this, then you can pick up the book I co-wrote with Monica, *Get Your Book Selling on Kickstarter*, from most major retailers.

Join paid group promos

If you're more passive in your marketing, then I would suggest you join some paid group promos on websites like Booksweeps because they will then go out and find you subscribers passively without you doing much of anything.

Cards on the table, I run ad-based builders with Booksweeps, so I'm biased. Their social-based ones are good but do require more effort. The ad-based ones allow you to pay the entry fee and get delivered a list once the promotion ends.

This is obviously less effective at conversion than somebody buying your books, but if you have a great automation sequence, then you can absolutely make this work for you.

You need an ***absolutely killer*** automation sequence to turn new readers into raving fans, along with a self-liquidating offer to help you bear the upfront cost, but if you can set these up, then this is really effective and easy. We teach you how to do all of this in our Direct Sales Accelerator.

Please note that automation sequences are not something you can do on Substack, so you would have to create a different account somewhere else to take full advantage of using this strategy effectively.

Organize an anthology

If you are somebody who doesn't like doing marketing at all, a very effective way to get subscribers is through organizing an anthology, either free or paid, and using the combined power of network effects to have all of you roll one boulder up the hill together.

Most people think the only outlet for an anthology is to put it up on retailers, but if you're looking for subscribers, you can just as easily gather writers for something you launch on a site designed to collect your email addresses or even as a free lead magnet in perpetuity.

This anthology series has provided thousands of new subscribers for my ecosystem while allowing me to grow my career exponentially.

You would have to use something like Kickstarter or BookFunnel, where you gather the emails to make this work, but it can be very effective to have everybody market to their little audiences to create a big audience.

I launched my career curating anthologies through projects like *Cthulhu is Hard to Spell* and *Monsters and Other Scary Shit*. I already had some small projects and some success before these launched, but the anthologies took me to another level.

Yes, I used this method for fiction, but there is no reason you can't do this for nonfiction. I've seen nonfiction authors who have tried to sell me into joining their sets for thousands of dollars, but you can absolutely do this for way less. You can also do this with course bundles, either for free or for a low price. I've been part of course bundles before, and they usually net a couple hundred new subscribers and a very little bit of money.

Also, please note that I used the word "organize" and not "edit". I did edit the first two of my anthologies, but I hired an editor for the last two I did, and now I have a publishing company that does basically everything for the series.

Join BookFunnel and/or StoryOrigin

If you want to gather a lot of good readers fast, then one of the best singular investments you can make is to get a BookFunnel account. Because almost every author uses BookFunnel, and because they are very meticulous on how to vet readers before they can sign up, when you join one of their group promos, you can be almost assured they are real people who like to read. Also, because they are signing up directly for your book, there is a high likelihood they are in your ideal audience.

I personally don't use StoryOrigin, but I know some authors love them, and they also have group promos. I know the owners of both companies, and they are good people. I just happen to know the owner of BookFunnel better, so I know more about their backend.

These group promos require a little more effort because you need to send them to your email list and (preferably) promote them on social media. However, I have gotten thousands of emails from BookFunnel over the years, and they have often become my best readers. Just note that they do give you a unique link, and your reputation is tracked by their system so others can see it when they decide whether to let you into a promo, so you actually do have to promote to keep getting approved for the best promos.

Just like above, you need a killer automation sequence and self-liquidating offer to make this work well, but it can be a great resource. On top of that, I use BookFunnel to host all my books, like the one you see above, and read a lot of them on their app, too.

Form a book club around your genre

My friend Andy Peloquin and I started the Action Fantasy Book Club with ten other authors. We offer a different author's book every month to members for free, but we're mostly promoting the book club.

We all chipped in some money and used that to get new subscribers. We collect all the emails and distribute them to the authors at the beginning of every month, then have a schedule for when we can add those readers to our list so they aren't all bombarded at once.

Note that we have every author listed on the sign-up page, and we explicitly state that subscribers will have their email distributed to all members.

Authors have to commit to marketing the book club for a whole year and agree to promote it at least once in their emails every month. In return, each author gets a highly curated list of readers who are interested in our niche genre.

Additionally, Andy and I are building the main list, which grows bigger every month and becomes an asset that compounds over time. Since January, we've built a list of over 5,000 email addresses, and we add hundreds more every month.

I have watched this work successfully in several genres. Again, while this is fiction, there's no reason why you can't use this same strategy in nonfiction or even journalism to make it work for you.

Round robins

Elana Johnson introduced me to this concept. You work with eleven other writers and every month, you promote a different person's work. Everyone cycles through the same list of people, so over the course of a year, you promote everyone else one time.

You don't have to spend a whole year implementing this, either. I've watched authors condense this strategy into a "week of awesome" or have a themed promotion like "travel cozy mystery week", where they promote a different book every day of a hyperfocused week instead of spreading it out over every month of a year.

This strategy is much easier to organize than starting a book club, but you are not building a compounding asset that grows more powerful every year. Also, there's no reason you can't use both of these strategies with different groups of authors.

This would work wonderfully with Substack's existing infrastructure, and a lot of writers already do this naturally. I follow dozens of writers who spotlight other Substacks through guest posts and backlinks every month, but doing it with intention would make it even more powerful.

You can also supercharge this strategy by adding in the recommendations that subscribers see after they sign up for a Substack. It would be relatively easy to cycle through different writers each month with a few minutes of work.

You really need to trust that the other writers will deliver, though. Don't agree to promote somebody else unless you are absolutely sure they can deliver the goods.

Exhibit at conventions

Even after 200+ events, I can still get hundreds of subscribers at conventions. If I really push, I can get 400-500 new subscribers at a big convention. Just know that it's very hard to get a ton of subscribers and also make a lot of money at a convention, so you should choose one or the other as your path to success going into an event.

Getting lots of subscribers at a small convention works best if you have something awesome to give away. I used to go around to other booths before the convention floor opened, ones I knew were good sellers, and put together gift bags of their most popular work. Then, I would do a free raffle at the end of every day for people who signed up while the floor was open.

I generally only use this strategy at slow shows, farmer's markets, and conventions with lower-than-normal foot traffic. Using this strategy, I could get 50-100 subscribers a day, even at a show with very low attendance.

Even if you don't do a giveaway, it makes sense to have a tablet to take down emails for people who aren't ready to buy yet. If somebody is about to walk away without purchasing, ask them if they would like to sign up for your list so you can send them some free samples of your work. This strategy works really well, especially at bigger shows with near-constant foot traffic.

If you're speaking at a convention, even if you're not exhibiting, then I highly recommend bringing a clipboard or two that you can pass around during your panel to gather emails. Just clear it with the other speakers before you pass around a clipboard to avoid looking rude.

We did this at 20Books Vegas last year and ended up with 400-500 new emails after all our panels. At the beginning of each panel/workshop, we stated that we had additional, targeted resources that we would send after the convention to people who signed up. Each list was hyper-focused on the topics we talked about, and they converted very well into paying students.

The great thing about conventions is that attendees have self-selected to be there and are very likely to make the effort to read your work. They are motivated to learn more about the topic of the convention, so if you choose the right ones, then you can really get far.

Just know that you likely need to be an outgoing sort of person or amazing at design to make this work well. If you just sit behind a table or stay silent on panels the whole time, then you're going to have a bad experience and waste your time. If you want to learn more about conventions, you can pick up our book, *Get Your Book Selling at Events and Signings*.

Set up your website to encourage subscribers

One of the biggest mistakes writers make is that they don't have ***a prominent way*** to sign up for their email list on their website.

Your site needs to feature ***a prominent giveaway*** at the top of the homepage and the footer of every page. Even if you don't have a book, a collection of your best posts or some other resource needs to be available to people first thing when they reach your site.

If you go to my website, I get 20-50 new subscribers every month just from having a big header with a lead magnet and a footer that offers a free book to everyone.

I know the scholarship is all over the map when it comes to having personal websites, but I've always believed it was essential to have a "home base" where everyone who types in your name into a search bar can find you easily.

I recently lost my Facebook account for reasons and went searching all my friend's websites to sign up for their email list. ***It was a dismal experience.*** Out of 100 or so websites I visited, I only found an easy way to sign up for their list on a few of them. I was very motivated to join their email list, and I literally couldn't do it. ***What a waste of my time and theirs.***

Most people are coming to your website to either read your bio, buy your books, or sign up for your email list. ***Make it easy for them.***

Get your back matter right

If you have books, then the one inch of space after the book ends is your prime real estate to get people to take action. Are you sending people to your list? Are you using your organic reach to sell the next book? Are you getting them to an offer on your website that is relevant to their interests?

Most authors do none of these things. Others do too many of them. Readers are generally only able to perform one, and only one, action. Don't overwhelm them, but do take advantage of that space by sending them somewhere before they come down from their book high.

If you have a Substack, does every post point back to a relevant offer on your website? When you do interviews on other platforms, are you saying, **"Check out my Substack"**, or are you saying, **"If you're interested in this topic, then I put together a special bonus about this topic, which you can find by heading to this special link."?**

The first one is okay for the few people who fall in love with you during the interview, but the second one is going to send the people you convinced to learn more on the topic to download your additional resources.

There will be many times people who want to learn more about a topic than fall in love with you during an interview, so using the second strategy will net you more email addresses and give you more readers to convert them into paid subscribers.

Even if you are a fiction author, you should be driving people back to the most relevant book with your content marketing. Even if you only offer a sample of a book, giving readers a specific call to action that is hyper-targeted to their interests will work better than just giving them a general website to check out.

The more specific and direct you are with your organic traffic, the more success you'll have in turning casual readers into subscribers. The more direct you can be in your marketing to those people, the more of those subscribers will turn into buyers.

"Go wide" with your work

Yes, you publish your work on Substack, but even if you only engage with people on Substack, then there's no reason why you can't distribute your content across the internet and point readers back to Substack if they want to form a deeper connection with you.

If you have more time than money, then you can make a hit list of social platforms that give the best bang for the buck in your genre and post to them yourself. I do recommend waiting around for an hour after you post just in case people have commented so you can help juice the algorithm to your advantage.

If you have more money than time, you can hire a VA to cross-post for you on different platforms.

If you write fantasy, then Royal Road and other serialized fiction apps are great for getting exposure and funneling people to somewhere else they can support you. If you write romance, then you can use sites like Radish to expand your reader base.

If you write nonfiction, simply posting the content (***not a link***) on social media will drive people to your site as long as you provide a strong call to action. No, it's probably not a ton of traffic at any one time, but my business partner talks about pennies in the bank, and that is what you're doing by going wide with your content. These little things compound over time, but it does take a significant amount of time to see the momentum build using this strategy, so it's better to use this in tandem with other strategies on this list that can help you grow faster.

Generally, doing interviews with other websites and creators, doing swaps of your stories to each other's audiences, and being in as many places as possible so people can find you the most places is an effective long-term strategy, even if any single piece of content doesn't move the needle much by itself.

I get people finding my work every day from work I put out years ago, which is kind of like past Russell being kind to future Russell, and above all, ***one of the chief principles in my life always is to try to be kind to future Russell.***

That said, I am all about conserving energy these days. I don't have active profiles on any social media platform, and I don't post on other sites. I have a mailing list, and I do interviews surrounding some of my bigger launches. Otherwise, I've cocooned myself to protect my precious energy, ***so if this sounds like a lot and it doesn't resonate, that's okay.***

Interacting on other posts and being helpful

Often, the best marketing is simply being pleasant, courteous, and helpful on other people's posts. This isn't about spamming your content or just saying, "Cool!". It's about having genuine and interesting deep interactions that help make people's lives better by you being part of it.

This method doesn't "scale" well, but one of my favorite pieces of startup advice is that to scale, you must do the unscaleable. Even to this day, I still make most of my best connections during spontaneous, one-on-one interactions with people.

I am confident that I make great books and write best-in-class articles, so by interacting with people and exposing them to my general vibe, I know the right people who resonate with my message are going to find something they like and check out my work. ***If they don't, that's okay.*** I still had a nice conversation, which has the benefit of making life less miserable just by the fact that it happened.

Using this as a "growth strategy" really only works if you have a strong voice and if you do it with no expectation of results. ***It seems like doublespeak to say that the only way to have results is not to expect results, but it's also true.*** You have to do this simply for the love of helping people and being a generally interesting human that exists trying to add light into the world that is too often filled with darkness.

If you start interacting with people expecting them to like or follow you, it's going to be a really bad time for you. People are very good at discerning genuine reactions from a marketing tactic. However, if you can do this because you want the interaction and you have a great ecosystem, then you'll be pleasantly surprised with how far this simple bit of advice can take you.

In fact, ***the best marketing is usually simple.*** It is augmented by a sometimes complex backend, but the actual act of marketing is pretty simple. It's interacting genuinely with people in interesting ways and building connections with them that resonate through time.

How to avoid getting lost in the flurry of new Substacks

There has been a lot of talk from newer writers on Substack about being drowned out by the recent flood of well-known authors like Junot Díaz, Margaret Atwood, Elizabeth Gilbert and many more who seem to have joined the platform in droves recently.

(All of whom I adore and subscribe to, so this is no shade on them on the minuscule chance they are reading this.)

Luckily, I've (Russell) got a lot of experience with this topic, specifically from my experiences on Kickstarter. During the pandemic, publishers like Boom Studios and Top Cow started using the platform while bookstores were closed, and they even joined with actors like Keanu Reeves to make seven figures on the platform.

Creators were not happy that they were taking focus away from them in the only place online they had where they could reasonably make money from their comics.

The influx of fiction authors like Brandon Sanderson created a new wave of this conversation on Kickstarter. However, it's a conversation that goes back to the dawn of publishing. Every time a celebrity gets a book deal, authors talk about the same type of thing.

Yet, writers survive in all this turmoil, and new authors do break through, even almost 600 years since the invention of the printing press and over 5,000 years since the earliest known uses of the written word.

One of the hardest parts of struggling against being drowned out by new, often more successful, voices is to accept that it will absolutely happen, and repeatedly, throughout your career.

It will happen at every level of your career.

No matter how often you rise to the top, you will be drowned out by more successful voices that have bigger, more established audiences.

I used to have an indie comics platform, which was relatively small compared to the indie publishing platform I have now.

However, my current platform is relatively small in the publishing community as a whole. The publishing community is relatively small compared to other creative industries, which are relatively small compared to overall entrepreneurship, which is relatively small compared to the entire working world, which is only a fractional share of the things people think about in their overall life on a daily basis.

Even the President of the United States spends an inordinate amount of time finding ways to rise above the noise and avoid being drowned out.

If we can come to terms with the fact that most of our career will involve the risk and certainty of being drowned out, then the best we can do is find how to swim with the current and gather buoys to help us float until we find an island.

Once we have an island, then we can fortify it against flooding and build structures that protect us as best as possible.

These include the audience we build, the work we make, and how we cultivate them in a nurturing way.

The things we can't control are how and when the floodwaters will rise.

What we can do is make sure we aren't building on a swamp or riverbed and then find ways to build structures that can survive the rough waters.

If we are really smart, then we will build a boat that can rise with the tides and bring us along for the ride.

I know many people who see marketing as a dirty word.

However, the way you get through these tough waters is to build an audience through marketing and attract the right people to you through your brand who want to support your work.

Marketing is really not a dirty word. Yes, it's sometimes a chore, but it's also how you gather fans who will lift you in the darkness. It is how we find purchase in the turbulent waters of creative entrepreneurship.

All of the fears you're feeling right now about falling further behind are imminently solvable, to some degree at least, but you have to learn how to swim out of your depths.

Marketing can teach you to swim. Sales can build a better boat, so you never have to feel that way again, and you can live in stillness. Let's talk about a few ways you can use marketing and community to build a boat in the storm.

If you are good about building your brand, then I'm not sure it matters if big names come onto a platform and disrupt things.

In many ways, if you are easily findable, it can be a great boon because they will bring their readers, and you can be caught up in the wave as they search for new publications to read.

In general, the top end of the market thrives with the introduction of big-name authors.

However, with those big authors comes increased visibility on the platform, which brings new authors who start writing on it.

For a mid-list or entry-level author, this can be devastating because a whole slew of new publications are vying for attention from a relatively stagnant reader base.

The rise of Amazon led to the demise of the mid-list authors as they were drowned out by indie books. Eventually, they either all moved indie, where they could get more traction, or they drowned.

As much as I like Substack, there is no doubt that their publications are growing much faster than their readership.

This floods the market with new writers and drowns out smaller publications that are trying to find readers from a stagnant pool of readers that isn't growing fast enough to support them.

I have seen this happen a lot during my career, especially with Kickstarter. The flood of new campaigns after authors like Brandon Sanderson and Sherrilyn Kenyon were a boon for the already successful authors.

However, the mid-list or smaller authors got killed if they couldn't find ways to stand out above the rising tide.

The worst part is that successful authors don't see it.

They don't often talk to entry-level authors or dig deep into their businesses to see what's happening. Authors generally talk to other authors at the same level, and everyone at their level is having a great time. So, they see these influxes as nothing but a boon.

Even as the younger authors drown, successful authors tell them there's nothing wrong, and they are imagining it.

But it is happening. It's just not happening to them.

On top of that, those newer authors look for advice on how to use platforms, so those already successful authors get a second boon by getting an influx of new readers from authors as well, trying to find purchase somewhere.

I won't lie, the influx of new authors to the platform has been great for my publication, which is all about growing your author business.

I am one of the more successful publications of its kind, so I get a good stream of new subscribers.

Even then, the flood of new publications has bumped me from 11th in my category to 20th, even as I've more than doubled my paid subscription base. ***That's a huge drop in just a couple of months.***

I will tell you this...smaller authors getting drowned out does happen. It ***is*** happening.

You are not crazy. I have seen it happen before enough times to notice the signs.

The good news is that these new publications mostly burn bright and then burn out. Something like 90% of publications don't make it past 10 articles.

Most of the new publications I subscribe to never post another article.

However, it feels gross to revel in that kind of thing. I want us all to win, and I think we can all win. It just takes more than it took before.

Things that worked in 2018, 2020, or even 2022 often don't work now.

A lot of those publications that succeeded got a boost from the first mover advantage, and looking at them for what works now is a serious case of survivorship bias.

If you are a newer publication, it is flat-out harder for you than it was even six months ago, especially right around the launch of Notes.

That time period was a gold mine around here. People who joined before then got ***huge*** boosts that you probably won't get.

If you want to succeed here, then it becomes about standing out from the crowd. How do you do that?

- **Associate with other authors in your genre who are doing good work**—Yes, this seems counterintuitive to what I just said, but curation is king in a flooded market. If you can associate with people doing good work, then you can all amplify each other. That is the reason salons historically worked so well.

- **Become a fulcrum for your niche**—If you are interested in getting even further ahead, you can create a salon of authors doing good work. You must be very choosy and make sure you all amplify each other, and sharing each other's work is a boon to all of you.

- **Make a world-class publication**—Yes, you can make any publication, but if you want to be shared, you must be shareable. There is an exponential growth curve if you can get to the top of your niche.

- **Leverage your work to do more with less**—The best part about marketing is that it allows you to do more with less. If you have a great publication and can get interviews on other blogs, then you are able to leverage that more because more people will go to your publication.

- **Be in the top 10 of your topic**—When you think about your niche, you need to be named in the top 10 of your topic. My old manager used to say, "If you're not in the top 10, then you might as well not be on that list". If you can't be in the top 10, make a new topic that you can dominate and become a fulcrum. I think you should aim for the top 3, not 10, but let's get to the top 10 first and go from there.

- **Share other articles you think your audience will like**—The minute your audience can associate you with other publications, they will put you in the conversation with those writers. You don't have to do a roundup like me, but you should be sharing and curating your feed so people know your point of view.

- **Have a strong point of view**—Substack is mostly about following a specific writer, and people follow others who have interesting points of view on the world. You can write about just about anything, but your point of view is everything.

- **Collective action will save you**—If you can build something with other people on the same journey, then you will all be able to amplify each other. People will be more likely to follow other people you recommend, and it will amplify your work. Just make sure they are people that cast you in a good light.

- **Understand you are building something with your readers and other publications in your niche**—While I talked about competing for eyeballs with every other publication, you are also part of a tradition. Together, you and other writers, along with readers, are building an ecosystem. People in your genre want to find other people who do the thing they do well and can help them build a stronger category.

- **Keep doing it**—If you keep doing it well, you will outlast most other people and eventually be noticed, as long as you keep doing interesting work and serving your audience.

You win by creating an environment of great publications and fostering it with readers and writers who are good stewards of it.

It's not easy. None of this is easy. And if you don't want to do it, that's fine. You don't have to do it, but you can do it if you want to do it. You can actually become one of the people who gets buoyed instead of the ones who are drowning.

People often ask me why they can't get other people to share their articles or work with them.

By people, they mean successful people, of course, and the first thing I tell them is that I bet there are hundreds of people at your level of success who would love to share your work.

Those are the people you should be networking with anyway because they are the ones most likely to pull you up when they rise, and vice versa.

Since I know that won't satiate you, I will let you know what I have observed, both building my own success and talking to others who are successful.

Do you want to know why? I'll tell you.

People ask a lot of successful people, they offer nothing in return, and they treat people with audiences as commodities.

This year has been eye-opening for me because, at some point along the way, I went from a human being to a commodity as I reached a certain level of success.

I'm not sure what triggered it, but a few months ago, I started to find much more negative sentiment around me in general, and that general sentiment treated me as if I wasn't an actual person.

It acted as if I was a printer, a dishwasher, or a large corporation instead of a human. I looked around and saw that a lot of my friends were treated the same way.

At some point, the general sentiment became "Russell is no longer a human, but a public figure that we can treat like any old ruddy thing."

And that's fine, I guess, people can people...then, the speaking opportunities came with greater frequency.

I tried to say yes to everything, but I just couldn't. Then, I started to realize that even the things I said yes to became transactional.

Last year, when I spoke, people always reached out afterward with a thank you. Now, people were treating me like my participation was expected. I am never thanked anymore for my work. People just expect it from me.

Still, whatever. That's the price of success. I guess the expectation that I will always deliver is a good thing, and it is nice to be asked. Energetically, though, I only have so much to give.

It's less nice when you politely decline, and they snipe at you, which also happens a lot. I feel pressured to say yes because otherwise, people think I'm a diva.

More so, they often want to charge people to listen to me speak and then don't want to pay me. The number of times I've said yes to an opportunity to speak, only to find out later that they are charging and not paying me, is staggering.

Everyone seems out to screw you, and those are the good-natured ones.

Then, the bad actors started to come out, trying to get me to endorse something or participate in one thing or another. They use that guilt of saying no to pressure you to do things for them.

Most of them are easy to spot, but some are well hidden, and it would take *a lot* to suss them out beforehand. While I would love to accept every possible opportunity that comes my way, unfortunately, sometimes bad actors come along and spoil it for everyone.

While I do love the attention, this isn't really about me but about how you act around and with successful people.

If you want to break through the wall they have up, it's actually pretty easy.

Treat them like a human and not a commodity. Do it repeatedly for a long time, long past the time when it would be financially beneficial to do so, and if you reach out to work with them, offer to pay a fair rate.

I remember when I started doing my roundup. I got a few responses, but most of the people I put into the newsletter, especially the super successful ones, didn't say anything.

Why would they? I was a new person, clearly trying to bank on their name.

But I didn't stop doing it. I kept putting them in my roundups (when they wrote a worthy article), and I didn't ask them for anything.

Slowly but surely, more of them started to come around, and now many of them comment on the roundup or share it.

I think it's because I've been doing it for months and I haven't asked for anything. The orange check mark by my name helps a bit now, too.

I don't want anything except for them to keep writing. The roundup isn't for them or even for me. It's for the readers.

I try to make my roundup a meritocracy. You are just as likely to get in with your first article as your 1,000th.

I've been doing this a long time, and every time I meet successful people, they have their guard up initially unless either they knew of my work before or I was introduced through somebody else.

It took proving I wasn't going anywhere, that I didn't want anything from them, and that I was interesting enough to be around before they dropped their guard.

It took showing them I didn't want to exploit them like most other people they met, and trust me, successful people are exploited constantly.

Over time it's become easier and easier to get people to drop their guard as I've gotten more successful and been around longer. Once they saw me as a good steward of the industry, most of them came around.

Some still hate me, though. I can't do anything about that. It's very hard to love somebody's work and have them not want anything to do with you, but that is just the way of things at every level.

I say all that to say this...the thing you say, complaining that somebody or another won't share your work, is treating them like a commodity, not a human.

That way of thinking is the exact reason why they won't do it and won't ever do it until you change the way you think.

Successful writers are not commodities. They are not corporations. They are humans who like being treated like humans.

I know you want those people to share your work to validate you or so they can transfer some of that success onto you, but success is not all it's cracked up to be in that respect.

I talk to a lot of unsuccessful authors, and the caution I give them is that success won't fix the hole inside of you, and it won't fix what you think is broken about you. It will just amplify it. Fast growth often brings more problems than solutions.

So, yes, success is good, but I also find almost everyone wants fast success for bad reasons that won't actually satisfy them. Slow growth and networking with writers at your level are usually more helpful than getting somebody successful to share your work.

More importantly, it's the way that is most likely to lead to the kind of success that will give you some stability in this very chaotic career path you've chosen.

One of the best ways to build your success and help craft a boat is to become a great content curator.

In today's information-driven digital landscape, content curation offers a compelling opportunity to provide value, cut through information overload, and build a loyal community. As a content curator, you can establish yourself as a trusted source of knowledge, foster relationships, and continually expand your expertise. By curating and sharing high-quality content within your chosen niche, you not only connect with like-minded individuals but also complement your content creation efforts, potentially leading to authority status and even monetization opportunities. Ultimately, content curation is a rewarding endeavor that requires dedication, a deep understanding of your audience, and a genuine passion for your chosen subject matter.

People ask me a lot how they can increase their output if they are slow writers, and I always tell them they should start to curate content for an audience. It takes 1-2 hours a week (as long as you are reading broadly in your field of study), and it's a great way to give back to the community.

Writers think they can only do this for nonfiction, but I built my fiction business by curating books and other content for fiction readers.

Once somebody knows you have good taste, they are more likely to follow you and buy your books. If you can show them that you like the same books they do and that you grok the same stuff, you will be well on your way to building a lifelong reader.

The key to curation is care, an almost single-minded dedication to surfacing what your audience needs to hear and what will enhance their lives.

You can push them out of their comfort zone if you find something they need to hear, but you have to know your audience well enough and be doggedly committed to enriching their experience.

I see a lot of people who do roundups because it's the thing to do, but they don't understand that curation has very little to do with what you like (though that is part of it).

It has everything to do with what will enrich your reader's experience inside your publication.

Like everything else, ***it's all about them.*** There are hundreds of articles I read a week that I enjoy, but I won't put in a roundup.

The perfect articles are the overlap between what you love and what you think your audience will love. That said, I've added articles that I don't love but speak to something my audience needs to hear. It happens less often, but it does happen as long as it's a well-written article.

I can tell the difference between objectively good and subjectively my jam, which is an important skill in any curation.

Ideally, they are a mix of articles they've seen a bunch online and haven't had a chance to read, as well as ones they have never seen but want to amplify.

Curation is an art. It's one of the best ways to show to somebody you have good taste and bring them deeper into your ecosystem, but if you don't have that level of faithfulness to your audience, it can easily backfire.

If somebody thinks you have their best interests at heart in all things, then they will be more comfortable going all-in on you until you break that trust, of course.

However, if you are haphazard with your curation, it can easily go the other way and turn people off.

My father taught me from a very young age all about countercyclical living. The main idea of it is that if there's a crowd there, go somewhere else.

We would always park a little further from the store, for instance, because it was easier to find a spot.

Or, instead of standing in line for hours to see a new movie (back before you could get tickets online), we would see a movie a few weeks later.

My father didn't understand why anyone would go where the crowd was when it was so much more pleasant to go the other way.

I'll be honest, it was infuriating when I was younger, but the older I get the more I see the wisdom in it.

This presents in business as the Blue Ocean Strategy. Most people focus on the red ocean, where "sharks" are constantly feeding and competing for money, but countercyclical living teaches us to go where people aren't and build our business there.

What does this have to do with not getting drowned out by the crowds? Well, it's pretty simple. ***If a bunch of people are drowning, you should probably not go that way.***

Instead, you should go another way and find shallower water. If everyone is talking about one thing, then you find another axis to talk to the same people about something different.

Yes, there is a benefit to going into the red ocean where everyone is feeding because that's where the action is, but plenty of people are completely turned off by that, and you can get by really well doing the opposite thing.

It might take a little bit longer, but the sea is calm, and you can go at a leisurely pace because nobody is there yet.

Then, when people figure it out and start a frenzy, either you jump to the next thing, like a Desert, or you've spent so much time there that you're now the first to feed, like a Grassland.

If you want to grow fast using this strategy, then you can harness your inner Tundra to draw attention to the thing you figured out and start a frenzy, but you can also go your own pace and keep the ocean calm.

People sometimes ask me why, since I talk so much about growth, I write things that have almost no virality potential, like my post this week about taking a break.

I tell them my secret, and most of them don't get it.

Now, I'm going to tell you why I do it, and maybe you will understand better than them, or maybe you'll think it's dumb, too.

I write about things people want to hear so they read the things they need to hear.

Certain posts are tailor-made for growth, namely when I talk about Substack. If you write about Substack, you will grow faster than writing about anything else.

That's great, but more important to me than growth is showing people how capitalism is destroying their mental health and how to live inside an oppressive system while still maintaining their artistic spark.

Those are not posts that get a lot of virality. They don't grow fast, but they hopefully ignite a spark in the people who need to read them.

This is a two-pronged approach to growth. I call it the Switch.

Get people into my publication with something easy to consume.

Feed them articles they need to hear to build a sustainable career.

I know the posts that people need to hear will likely shrink my audience, so they must be combined with posts designed to make it grow.

It is this process that makes my publication a living organism that breathes in and out as it grows and shrinks.

It might be a dumb strategy, but it works for me. I have found it a great strategy to get large groups to talk about difficult topics.

People who make it through those difficult articles become my best subscribers. Those are the articles that change lives, but they need to subscribe to my publication to do it.

If you follow my work, you probably found me through my growth articles and hopefully stick around for the rest of it. Every publication I have ever paid for, including the Washington Post, had a flashpoint article where I started to pay attention, a building effect where I learned about what they were about over several different axes and a tipping point article that convinced me to pay for a subscription.

Usually, the article that made me subscribe was very different from the one that made me pay attention, and both of those articles are different from the one that made me fall in love with their work.

I should note that I love every type of article I write for my publication, but they have different purposes.

If you don't want to be on social media, you can start doing paid ads and get the same effect, or hire somebody to do it for you.

If you don't have money for paid ads or to hire somebody, you can do the work yourself and be on social media.

...This is the cyclical conversation I go through with most of my clients when we get started.

You'll be investing either money, time, or both. You can't get through that. No, there's not somebody who will work on performance for a person that isn't proven.

You either have to pay somebody to do it, pay an algorithm to do it, or do it yourself. The less you want to do, the more you have to pay.

The goal is to make enough to pay for the advertising/help and make a profit. Meanwhile, you get to do the things you like more, and hopefully, you will be able to be more productive, which will help you make even more.

I wish the world worked differently, but you either have to pay capitalism in time or money.

This stuff is very hard to hear and even harder to implement. It's likely that it prickled, maybe even rankled you, so I want to provide some final guidance on this topic.

1. **I never claim that my advice is guaranteed to work for you.** I have studied thousands of successful creators, interviewed hundreds, and experimented in my own business with what they told me. The advice I give is the best practices I found by trying to systematize what I saw and bring it to you. It is not a personal attack on you. My interest is mainly in the sociological impact of how groups of people operate successfully, focused through the lens of what worked for me.
2. **Sometimes, you have to do things better.** In fact, most of this is about figuring out how to do things better over time. I have no idea where your business is, but when I dig into why people are failing, most of it is about them not doing things well enough. Their books don't look good enough. The writing isn't tight enough. They need to uplevel their network. They need to get better at marketing. Their website requires more work. They need to put more people into their funnel. I have written hundreds of thousands of words in defense of this throughout this publication. I have no idea why a single person is failing unless I dig into their business. However,

usually, almost every time, they need to do things better. That is a very hard thing to hear, but it is also true.

3. **If you want to be shared, you need to be shareable.** The #1 thing that prevents me from sharing something is that it's not ready for prime time. It's very hard to put on your reader hat and go, "Would I share this if I saw it?". I work with writers all the time who can't see their own blind spots, but I always ask them, "If you saw this out in the wild, would you share it?". They almost always tell me no. As readers, we all know when something is good. We just can't embody that person very easily. Critique groups are essential for young writers, and I don't see why there can't be ones here, too.
4. That said, at the end of the day, we all have to be better at putting our reader hats on and evaluating our work.

The harsh truth is that businesses are hard. 90% of them fail in the first year. 99% of them fail in the first ten years. On a long enough time horizon, almost every business fails, even if it's a hundred years later.

There are almost no businesses left that started in the 1800s, or even the 1950s, or even the 1990s.

Almost every one of them, even if they were once enormous, has failed or been absorbed by another company.

This is especially true in creative businesses like writing. There is so much competition, and it's so hard that almost everyone gets drowned out at some point. Sometimes, people get drowned out for years or decades and then make a glorious comeback.

This does NOT mean you are not good enough. You are good enough. However, growing a business is very different. It's not personal.

Growing a business is not really about you at all. ***It's how you make other people feel about their own lives.*** You have to be able to project outward and imprint on other people, and most people are really bad at that.

There are ways to do it that are more likely to lead to success. They might not lead to your success. I'm just sharing things that have worked for groups of other people that have found success.

Not being good at this stuff does not mean you are not good enough or that you don't deserve to be here.

You deserve to be here. You deserve to be here even if you never want to monetize.

You deserve to be heard. You deserve to be heard if only a few people hear you right now.

However, if you want to get to the next level, especially if you've been around for years or decades, and you're still not where you want to be, you have probably been doing things wrong, maybe for a long time.

There might be some shame there, or some anger that other people have passed you, or bitterness because you trusted other people to grow your business, and you feel that they led you astray.

I'm not sure, but I didn't do that to you, and I won't be a vessel for your anger. I will block you with impunity because I have boundaries.

You have probably been doing the same wrong stuff for years. Or maybe you're not doing those things well enough.

There is no shame in that. Other people shoot past you because they have learned and grown and figured out ways to project outward on other people in a way that resonates with them.

Maybe you don't want to do those things, and that's cool too, but you have to give up that anger and stop beating yourself up for not getting there. You have to let it go because if you're not doing the actions to get there, you'll never get the result.

This is really hard, but it's even harder to look around you and see if your writer friends are an anchor or a sail.

I know you love your friends and the people that you are around, but it's possible if you aren't where you want to be, it's because the people you hang around don't want to grow or they aren't ready to grow.

You really are the average of the five people you spend the most time with, and it's really hard to look at things like that. Still, if you want to get to the next level, you need to be around people who are all headed in the same direction and are committed to getting to the next level and the level after that.

Some people will want to come on that journey with you, but others will not be ready or willing to make that jump.

Maybe the people you are around are vampires, sucking your energy and taking from you without giving anything back. That is sad, but unfortunately, it happens all the time. Often, your network is holding you back, not pushing you forward.

This feels super tough to hear, I know, but it's not a personal attack. It is what I have found across studying this stuff for over a decade.

I don't want this stuff to be true. I want the world to exist in a different way, but it does not. We are all trying to change that world, but we also have to operate inside this world while we work to change it.

I tell people all the time, "You can try to fix the problem and complain all you want, or you can decide not to fix the problem, and then you can't complain. I don't really care which."

By try, I don't mean "throw anything at the wall". I mean, look at the instructions from an expert and follow them. Even then, if I have a Samsung washing machine and I read the instructions for a KitchenAid mixer, I'm not going to complain to Samsung that it didn't work.

Nothing is a quick fix, but some things are generally true.

- Bet on people, not companies.

- Choose a group you want to serve, and then serve them long enough that they overcome the feeling that you will abandon them.

- Find ways to add value: monetarily, emotionally, mentally, and physically.

- The right people want to support you, not hold you back.

There are tons of ways to succeed, and none of them are quick, save for unplanned luck.

Quick money usually makes you feel gross. Good money comes from being a sail, not an anchor.

***

With Sparkle—I adore collaborating—there are so many adjacent niches for me to choose from on Substack. I push for one collaboration a month and have connected with so many wonderful colleagues from doing this. I'm two seasons into my podcast and have had some brilliant guests from best-selling authors to content creators and from artists to space holders—this all models how I am able to stay creative on Substack and encourages others to do the same. It builds the know, like, and trust factor, and it drives new subs. The colleague relationships I've built on Substack deepen month on month—it's a very special place to build relationships. Celebrate other people's work, reach out, ask questions, lean in, and model new ways of using the platform, from guest posts to audio and video collections—it's all yours for the taking.

Blog on Substack with Sparkle

I (Claire) wanted to write about using Substack as a 'blog' because the energy here has often been described as very 'old school' blog energy.

Blogs take the pressure off somehow...they can be experimental and shift topics as often as we change our socks! We don't have to be a pro writer to have a blog.

They can also be PLAYFUL. Want to write about your love for tiny penguins? Go for it. Want to call it Sky Blue Flamingos at Dawn? Ok then!

Writing on Substack is Storytelling

This is such an interesting topic for me BECAUSE I see the potential in Substack to be either a blog, a mailing list, or both.

Quite simply, it's a space for the stories you want to tell.

There's also a sneaky, relatively unknown secret in that you can start to create and write here without telling a soul...

Do you know people here? Maybe a handful? What a delight that is after being under a social media microscope for our whole career.

Why would you want to create without eyes on your work, I hear you ask?

Have you ever been to a retreat? Have you noted ideas down in your journal on a 'lazy' Saturday afternoon? Have you furiously free-written and read it back and thought, wow, there's something in that? Have you daydreamed about being a global bestseller one day?

Your creative heart needs SPACE! You can have that here.

Yes, Substack is the internet, but it's also a space where you can turn your light on to a soft, warm glow and give yourself time to rekindle your creative voice.

Want to write about work, love, life, memories, or a brand-new topic? Great!

Want to delete it after 24 hours? Fine!

Want a pen name to be discovered anew? Now we're talking!

Unless you have professional writing experience or FEEL like a writer, you will need to write a fair few words OUT of your system before you start a new phase.

This is what blogs were used for back in the day; they didn't show up as fully formed, well-researched essays; they just showed up.

Want to write out a recipe for your Grandma's fruit scones and link it to a poem about when you waited for a bus? Lovely!

You might write 'too much' or 'too little', and then it's 'just right'.

It's a feeling that you're home safe and that it's okay to thread words, art, and creative ideas together in a way that makes sense to you.

Embodied experience...

I've always written for work, funding bids, project plans, and arts sales copy.

I started writing blogs while working for New Writing North in 2014. I was a crap writer, technically, but it didn't matter. I started, and I committed to communicating what it was I had to say 10 years ago.

Now, my words are read by people in 90 countries here, and I've published four creativity and business journals. Those earlier blogs were an experiment...let's not mention the one I called 'Run with your heart, not with your legs'.

My current website doesn't have a built-in blog function, which is ONE of the main reasons I started writing over at Creatively Conscious right here on Substack back in April 2022. Quite simply, my company is called Creatively Conscious, and I wanted a blog space with the same name. I didn't move my mailing list until much later.

I also wanted to explore topics outside of 'typical' business-style blogs. I wanted space to re-discover my creative voice outside of a 'professional' environment.

A playground for words!

Having URLs of your work to share on other platforms is SUPER useful.

Think sharing on:

- LinkedIn.
- Instagram stories.
- Facebook groups.
- In another Substack post...
- On your website.

- On a link in your Instagram bio.

And it's completely FREE to start a "blog" here on Substack.

Me and Blogs; the back catalog

Back in 2022, I could NOT face logging into my WordPress site. It was so clunky and cluttered, and things were always breaking; the text was re-formatting, and I didn't really know what ads were popping up. Oh, my days of plug-ins and rogue bullet points—WHAT a headache! I was so busy with arts project management and commissions I had no time or inclination to keep fixing it.

Thankfully for all of us...

A Substack blog is CLEAN, easy to design, and there are NO adverts—yay!

I've since taught over 6000 people how to use Substack as a mailing list, blog, and platform for creative work. The thing I hear the most from my 1-2-1 clients and members here is that Substack is overwhelming.

The second thing I hear is about indecision about how to use it. The third is that it can feel a little elitist.

I'm going to speak to the first point first.

You can always 'Stay Creative' on Substack!

Substack is ever-evolving.

When I first arrived, I had a year of experimenting here without 'Notes' 2, and I was very much just having a nice time writing and creating. When Notes was introduced, things shifted and changed. We had an instant connection, flashes of problem-solving, and boatloads of opinions.

Rapidly, Substack rolled out a lot of new features. Knowing this is helpful, but you don't have to use them all or even want to. The way Substack existed before Notes, chat, video, etc., worked great and still does! This is why I push the 'stay creative' message so much. It's EASY to start a Substack. It's not so easy to write a strategy for yourself on how to continue.

Use Substack in the way that works for you. You don't have to enter the echo chamber anywhere online—create for yourself and your people will find you.

But what should I do first? How do I do it, and how long does it take?

This is where the croissant and coffee analogy comes in.

There's a store in the UK that offers a free coffee with a loyalty card. There's another that offers a free croissant. Technically, just for doing your grocery shopping in both stores, you could get a free coffee and a free croissant most months.

Your subscribers are simply people reading your blog who decide to invest their time in pressing subscribe in the hope that you'll keep providing the lovely free croissants and coffee.

If you don't, nothing BAD is going to happen. They will still be there waiting to visit your Substack when you're ready to publish. They are not saying; hey, I had a free coffee, and now I want one every day, and it must be this exact temperature. No, they are patiently waiting and going about their day. They are not thinking about when you're going to post again.

The reason I chose this analogy for Substack is that I don't know anyone who has gotten their "free" coffee and/or croissant and has not spent more time in these stores and spent more money with that particular chain.

If you offer valuable ideas (good coffee), people are going to return. They might even stay longer and read more of your work (and eat your croissants)...

How much time do you have? Some suggestions for you and a gentle strategy for you...

- 0-1 hours a week? Just enjoy being on Substack as a reader for a while. Read what lights you up. Don't follow anyone who upsets your flow. Yum!!

- 1-2 hours a week? You could start a blog here and start building your email list if you'd like. Keep the design simple and just write. You can faff on with all that later. People will sign up to receive your words; that's what happens here, especially if you add value and nourishment to their lives. Keep writing, see what chimes, and check your engagement stats. Don't know what to write? Write about the last time you 'felt' something...

- 2 hours+ a week? Same as above, but perhaps think about spending some time on Notes, too. Lean into how it feels to 'be' there with your creative colleagues. What conversations do you want to join in with? Are you ready to collaborate? Perhaps there's a chocolate croissant on the menu. Perhaps you've got too many croissants, and you want to pass some on.

- 3 hours+ a week or more? You could look at building the rest of your Substack system: design, recommendations, podcasts, design, audio, welcome emails...

Substack supports you to grow your subscriber base. Once your Substack is set up, you can comfortably follow the suggestions above week in and week out, and if your work is read by one person, it will soon be read by more.

What I'd advise is to keep track of your work in a planner or diary and reflect on how it's felt at the end of each month; it's really that simple.

I have one for sale here designed to hold your whole 2024 on Substack.

If you want eyes on your work, you'll need to use the Substack network either through Notes, the Substack Recommendations tool, or your own external networks/adverts.

Great work here finds an audience and is shared in multiple ways.

I don't feel part of "the party".

This is such a tough one, and I have heard and do hear it a lot. I work with best-selling authors who have imposter syndrome and stage fright. Writer's block haunts them throughout their projects; we all struggle.

Throughout my career, I've supported international award-winning artists and celebrities who feel sick to their stomach at the thought of PR. You are not alone; there's a really human need for us to feel accepted; your body's inbuilt warning system is trying to help. We have to lean into a new practice.

Substack wants you to succeed—they are growing this platform and their business. You can turn on these little cheerleading emails.

3 tips and ideas to support your journey in growing your Substack if you feel ready

- **Invite like-minded people to YOUR Substack party.** If you're feeling brave, start a community post or thread in Notes. You'll get out what you put in. Writers on Notes are your colleagues, your peers, and your equals. Treat them that way. Don't tag a 'celeb'; they probably won't reply.

- **Join a community where participation is encouraged.** I love Suzy Walker's Heart Leap and Things Worth Knowing with Farrah Storr, who both generously hold space for lots of us. Suzy and Farrah are both professional journalists, and they know the power of their members 'meeting' in their space on Zoom and in comments.

- **Stay in your lane for a while.** If comparison is going to creep in anywhere online, you can guarantee it will here. Write your blogs, post them to your Substack website, and have a lovely time. I'd advise writing at least 10 before you consider how to reach others because having eyes on your work is a whole other dynamic, so why not just enjoy the spacious creative void?

Top Tip for Blogging on Substack 'first'

As you are building confidence here, leave the delivery box unchecked; that way, you have a blog. You're writing a blog that can be viewed here but not sending it to an email list of subscribers...

To publish your posts as a blog, just don't tick either of these buttons when it comes to publishing. Obviously, if you don't have email addresses attached to your Substack, it won't go anywhere.

In my honest opinion, you'll probably be more tempted to check the box because 'why not?' only good things happen if you check that box—trust me!

If you don't, then write 5-10 and see what your views are looking like. Reflect on how it's feeling and what you want to do next.

How to compile your blog into a book

I've (Russell) released three solo nonfiction books up to this point in my career, all of which paid members can read for free:

- *How to Build Your Creative Career* (2017).
- *How to Become a Successful Author* (2019).
- *Advanced Growth Tactics for Authors* (2022).

Since I talk about them often, you might know they exist, but did you know that the last two books on this list were compiled almost exclusively through repurposing blog articles and Facebook posts?

Additionally, I'm working on a book called *How to Survive as a Writer in a Capitalist Dystopi*a, which will be mostly comprised of bits I worked out on this publication, too.

Even *Direct Sales Mastery for Authors* was mainly compiled of bits from *The Author Stack*, at least my portion of it, although for that book, I knew what we needed and was writing the pieces we needed in public.

For the other four books, though, I didn't quite know there would be a book or what that book would be when I set out to write the content for them.

In fact, I only intended to write one nonfiction book in my whole career (*ha!*), but people kept asking me for more, especially for a book specifically aimed at authors. Since I was writing a daily blog at the time called The

Complete Creative, it made logical sense to start with the information I had compiled there.

Then, three years later, my Facebook account was blinked out of existence. Luckily, I had a backup of all my best posts and could compile another collection of my best work.

From those books, I developed a system for bringing my blog content into a book format that might be a good template for you to follow.

It's important to note that I write a lot because it's how I process the world. I don't expect anyone else to write as much as me, but writing is how I self-soothe. I generally write fiction to have control of a world when it feels too chaotic to manage. I write nonfiction to process things I see in the world and make sense of concepts noodling around my brain. I don't feel like I really understand an idea until I finish a piece about it.

You might only have enough content to make a book every five years or ten, or you might be able to do it every year. There is no right or wrong here; it's just advice that might work for you.

Stage 1: Gather everything into one place

The first step to compiling a book is to get it off your blog to live in another document.

Personally, I like using Microsoft Word for this part of the process because I'm a fossil living in the past. I know Scrivener, Plottr, Atticus, and other programs make it easier to do this work, but I like Microsoft Word because it's what I know, and my brain is wired to think using its functionality.

I appreciate that Word allows me to see all the headings and subheadings in the left-hand sidebar. This is very important to the next part of my process.

Whatever platform you choose, ***the first step is to manually transfer everything from your blog into this new document.***

"But Russell," I hear you say. "Why can't I just export the whole thing into a document?"

Because the whole point is to create high touch points with your work. By manually transitioning each piece, it forces you to read and think about it. In doing so, you'll find articles that don't represent your best work, and you can cut them immediately. If you do this automatically or without intentional thought, it will disrupt this immensely important part of the process. ***This is not a process to optimize. The process is the point.***

When you get further into building this document, you'll start seeing how certain articles could be placed together to maximize impact. We don't usually write a blog in sequential order, so this is the first chance we have to impose order on chaos. Don't fight the urge to group similar things into what we call "buckets". Having 3 to 5 good buckets of like-minded bits and bobs will really help you move forward.

It wasn't until I started compiling this sequence that a theme emerged meaty enough to warrant being considered a book. Finding the thematic throughlines by reading your work again in short order and curating only the best things is what we're after with this process.

This kind of work takes as long as it takes. Don't hire an editor yet or have AI replace you to do this work. Once you're done, we'll have what they call in the movies an "assembly cut".

It's supposed to be awkward and clunky right now. We'll refine it in future stages.

Stage 2: Bringing order to chaos

At this point, you have a book or at least the makings of one. When I do this work, I usually end up with 100,000+ words at this point, and that's okay. We'll be cutting it down to 50-80k through the next part of the process.

From here, we will develop focus. Whether you're working in nonfiction or fiction (yes, you can do this with a short-story collection as I did with the forthcoming *Bulletins at the End of the World*), there should be a clear theme developing in your compiled work.

In the last stage, you began the process of grouping like topics into buckets. In this section, we will fine-tune that process. *Did you pick the right buckets? Do you have too many of them? How do they feel to you looking at them together? Does it make narrative sense?*

If you work in nonfiction, especially self-help or business, these buckets could start to form a framework for your whole teaching practice. If you already have a teaching practice, then your buckets should map into the 3-5 pillars of your framework.

In *How to Build Your Creative Career*, there were five buckets:

- Making Great Content.
- The Basics of Sales.
- Building an Audience from Scratch.
- Making a Profit at Live Events.
- Launching a Successful Kickstarter.

This book was written over five years ago, but it still acts as the pillar of my teaching modalities even today.

In *How to Become a Successful Author*, there were three:

- Mindset.
- Writing.
- Marketing.

During this process, you want to cut everything that doesn't fit your buckets and eliminate duplicate posts that double up on the same concepts too closely. Conversely, if you think both pieces are strong, you might consider merging pieces into one more powerful piece instead of eliminating one of them.

We all have recurring themes in our work we often don't see until we look at them together in one place. If you've never done this kind of work before, it should help you find some of the universal themes you keep coming back to in your work.

I'm a huge fan of mixtapes, and I have strong feelings that any good mixtape tells a story and has a narrative flow. I believe every good album has a narrative flow (and that we are currently in the best album era in all of human history. ***It is one of my hottest takes).***

Similarly, every good book compilation has a narrative flow that takes people on a journey. Regardless of the format, your job is to create and then deliver a transformation in your readers. ***If you don't know the transformation of your compilation yet, you have some work to do.***

The transformation you deliver raises your book above a compilation into something that will endure for years and become beloved among those who read it.

Once you finish with this part, you should have cut at least $1/5^{th}$ of the story down into a "rough cut", but you could cut as much as $1/3^{rd}$ of the book. That's okay and totally normal. It's not about the ***quantity*** of the words in your book. It's about the ***quality*** of the transformation you deliver.

If you're having trouble with either of the two bits above, you should think about hiring a developmental editor to help you find the vision and narrative flow of your story.

Stage 3: Filling in the gaps

Once you finish honing your buckets and find the narrative flow of your book, you will likely discover that there are gaps in the narrative that need to be filled to deliver a cohesive experience to your readers.

This is where a great editor can be super helpful. In *How to Become a Successful Author*, my long-time editor realized that in the writing section, I hadn't written anything about working with an editor. So, I had to write that part to complete the section.

In *Direct Sales Mastery for Authors*, Monica found gaps we failed to cover throughout our previous 20 books. So, we set out to write all of that material to fill in the story and deliver on our transformation. ***Don't try to fit a round peg into a square hole by keeping something that doesn't fit. Just write something new to fill in the gaps.***

This kind of fill-in work happens all the time with short story collections. Once writers and editors find the narrative thread and settle on the themes they want to tackle, they will often realize they are missing certain key elements that tie the story together and have to write something new to satisfy readers.

Even though we're building a compilation filled with seemingly disparate elements, we are still telling a story here. The sequence of those elements and the way in which they build out the story are what make it resonate as a cohesive hole.

People always ask about naming conventions for a compilation, but just like anything else, that comes when the narrative becomes clear. If you don't have a name by now, then you probably missed something critical in Stage 1 or Stage 2.

Once you finish filling in the gaps, you definitely want to hire an editor to make sure you didn't miss anything, or at the very least, bring it to a reader group or beta readers to make sure it delivers for them.

Stage 4: Tightening everything up

By this point, you might have jettisoned up to half your pieces to find the right narrative, and it's really starting to feel like a book. You could have had to rewrite some sections, add in more examples, or weave a meaningful personal journey between your pieces that moves the book along, but by now, it should feel like a cohesive piece instead of disjointed and disparate pieces.

If you're still having trouble weaving the narrative together and making your piece feel like a singular whole, here are some strategies you could employ to help you.

- Create a framework based around a work or concept, like Tim Ferris in The Four-Hour Workweek.
- Create a narrative thread around your personal journey, like Sarah Ramey's *The Lady's Handbook for Her Mysterious Illness.*
- Take us on an actual journey, like Elizabeth Gilbert in *Eat, Pray, Love.*
- Create a narrative weaving around and through your short-story collection, like Neil Gaiman in *The Graveyard Book.*

Building a narrative between the elements of your story can help create a connection with your readers. It's not necessary, though. If you've grouped your pieces well and they tell a nice, compelling story, you can create a great book without one.

Most of the rest is tightening your story to make sure it resonates with readers the right way. You might have to rewrite specific sections for narrative flow or add more examples to flush out your transformation. Your editor, writer's group, and beta readers should be able to help you get there, too.

Even though your book is a compilation of your blog, it's really a translation of your blog into a book, so it can and should feel a bit different than the original source material.

What you're trying to do is thread all these disparate throughlines into one cohesive narrative that delivers for readers. It's your job at this stage to thread and weave it all together into something that makes sense.

Why would anyone buy it if they read it on my blog?

By now, this should be obvious, but let's say the quiet part out loud. Readers will buy your book even, ***and often because*** they read it on your blog because the transformation is totally different!

There are just too many examples of writers who've done this successfully, from Allie Brosh to Jenny Lawson (AKA thebloggess), that I think we can definitively say it can, does, and will work. Still, it takes more than dumping your blog into a Word document and hitting publish.

Maybe that will get your existing audience, but even they want more. If you're going to reach a wider market, then you'll need to put a lot more effort and intention behind your compilation. It requires finding a deep, resonant transformation and delivering it well to get people to love your book, and that transformation is totally different than reading a post on your blog.

People who read pieces by way of disparate blog posts will have an entirely different experience when they see it all laid out in an order that builds on each other. They might have a little lightbulb go off, but it won't land for them until you tie it together for them in a cohesive narrative that works.

I'm a huge fan of both Allie and Jenny's work. I read their blogs for years before their books dropped, and I had a completely different, more transformative, and better experience with the books than their blogs because of how they weaved the stories together.

It's the same reason people buy courses or consulting when they can get the same information from a book. ***The transformations are completely different, and that's okay.***

Even I, the ***writer*** of my books, find a more powerful transformational impact reading my work as one coherent piece than when I originally wrote it for my blog. Often, things I barely realized the first time slap me in the face once they're all laid out in one place, and connections make sense in a way I never thought about before I bound them together in a book. ***In fact, I don't stop editing until I can see that impact in myself, just like I get for readers.***

If I can have that kind of transformation by reading my work in the right order, I promise your reader will as well. Additionally, people don't like searching through a complicated and messy blog to find the one piece they want to cite. They want it bound in one handy place for them. People pay for convenience, and having everything in a single, neat, convenient place is very handy.

Finally, and maybe most importantly, people want a totem they can share with their friends and people who matter to them to affect the same change in them that they got from you. Sending them to a blog is just not as satisfying as putting a book in their hands.

At the end of the day, a blog compilation is really just a book, and, really, what you're doing is creating a new experience out of your work that can deliver a bigger, more powerful transformation for your readers.

What if you don't want to make a book?

This is still a good exercise for your own Substack growth, even if you don't want to turn it into a book.

I've identified four main stages of Substack growth during my time on the platform. These are very broad categories, but pretty much every human I know has gone through them at one point or is currently in one of them.

1. **Figure out your publication.** Spend as long as you need to write whatever, flit around, pretend, explore, get good, and futz around. Don't even worry about a name yet. Just start and call it whatever.
2. **Rebrand.** A publication almost always has to rebrand once they figure their stuff out, so don't worry about your name at the beginning. You'll have time to get it right once you're ready to get it right. I had two that I can remember. I started as Wannabe Press, then went to Author Ecosystem, before finally ending up with Author Stack (and am currently fiddling with another thing that might change my branding again, though not for the main publication).
3. **Lay out your case.** This is the one most people miss, jumping straight from stage 2 to stage 4 and missing a big part of the growth pattern. Once you know what you want to say, you should go through a 3-6 month period where you lay out your case with long essays and other cornerstone pieces that you can drive people back to whenever they find you. These are critical pieces because people will come to your publication from random places, and you need to be able to give them something to latch onto and let them know they are in the right place. Not every post should be this kind of content, but over time, you'll build it out until it's lush. It should also be said that you might need several cases. I think I've built out 3 different cases since I've been on the platform: Author Ecosystems, How to Thrive as a Writer in a Capitalist Dystopia, and How to Build a World Class Substack. Each of these "cases"

became the books we talked about earlier, but they started as Substack collections.

4. **Push forward.** Once you have your case built, then it's time to push forward and keep writing about the things you like. Who knows? Maybe you'll need to rebrand again.

While this is ideal with an education or culture publication with a tight niche, even if you have a random, memoir, or fiction publication, the third part needs to be done so people feel like they know you or your story.

So many people simply never do the work of grounding people in your "theory of the case". If you can figure out your stance on life, love, and the pursuit of happiness, then it can only help you focus your voice as you move forward.

Short-circuiting the Substack burnout cycle

It seems like writers have a six-month burn rate where they come in excited, start to build, grind, and finally burn out. I've watched this cycle happen 2x now since I've (Russell) been studying it hardcore for a little over a year.

Of course, it's really happening constantly as people come onto the platform randomly. There is an almost daily crest and trough of it, but I've witnessed it with people I came up with 2x, starting in February 2023, cresting in June, and then burning out in August. Then, a new crop of people starting in August, peaking in December, and burning out in February/March.

Even if people bounce back once, they burn out again and harder until they are consumed in bitterness fueled by exhaustion and break the wheel. Every cycle gets more vicious as more and more people pile on, even if they are in the minority. Since more and more people burn out every day, often leaving the platform in protest, the vocal minority grows even if the majority of people are widely happy with the platform as a whole.

Did you know that historically, newsletters have rarely ever been self-monetizing? They have historically been things we built to monetize other things, such as books, courses, etc.

Knowing this, we would go into launch mode when something was coming out, but otherwise, our lives weren't filled with constant thoughts of how to make sure our paid subscriber count kept going up.

We could even say, "I just had a launch, and now I'm going to disappear for a couple of weeks", without worrying the universe would implode while we were gone.

I'll admit, recently, I've been pulling my punches, a bit scared that somebody will cancel their membership, and I never felt that way before, even when the same amount of money was on the line. I don't like it. I feel like I'm on stage at all times and that people think they should have constant access to me, even though nobody has ever said as much, and y'all are lovely and supportive in every way.

Always feeling like you are center stage is kind of awful. There's a reason actors only do it for a couple of hours a night and start to seem a bit crazy when they get too famous. When you feel like you have no private space and will always be judged, it makes you a bit messed up in the head.

That's not to say the launch cycle is much better. You are constantly either living in abundance or poverty, with the next launch always determining your mood. I've lived in the other model, and I like both for different reasons.

The fact that we have so many different ways for people to support our work and find what they need is kind of cool, like saying, "It's okay if you don't want my subscription, buddy. I'll have a book soon, or a conference, or some other way for you to get at me if you like my stuff".

That part's cool. I dig that, and I dig subscriptions because you can plan better for the future. There is a power in having recurring revenue coming in, but not if you're beholden to it. ***If you can't walk away or approach it with joy, then that makes it little more than a bad job and (usually) not a particularly well-paying one.*** It also means you are in constant launch mode, worrying only that the "line goes up" and reducing people to little more than a $20 bill, which is about the worst thing you can do to feel good about your author business.

I love Substack in many ways, but it seems like every move they are making is about increasing their valuation, not their actual value. For instance, while

DMs might be nice for some people, almost everyone I talk to thinks it is, at best, a net-neutral improvement. In contrast, we've been asking for better newsletter functionality for years now and, aside from audio and video functionality, haven't seen much of anything on that front.

The things they are adding seem tailor-made to make us feel like we must appear and perform every minute of the day, too, which is also a function of subscriptions in general, as you're constantly worrying about bringing in new subscribers and watching existing subscribers cancel their subscriptions.

Previously, launches could be bad, books could be bad, products could be bad, but that could be separated from the overall quality of the rest of our business. Now, it feels like everything is wrapped up in the strength of one stream of income.

So, I want to tell you right here, stop. Quit it.

Your moral worth is not dictated by the success of your newsletter, and it's certainly not dictated by the paid success of your newsletter.

Additionally, while it's great to have focus, it's better to have intention beyond money.

What do I mean by that? Well, I have quite a large number of subscribers by many metrics, and I've made a considerable amount of money...

...but the money is in service of creating new things, and the audience is in service of doing cool things.

I own a conference now, a publication I care about that you're reading now, a publishing company, and a training academy, among other things. I get to bring new voices into my publication that other people can enjoy. I wrote a comic with one of my favorite humans and one of the top writers on the planet. I'm starting a podcast with another one, a company with a third, and working closely with a fourth.

Everyone I meet now inspires me more than the last, but the last thing the audience brought me was money. Mainly, what they afforded me was access, and that access allowed me to make cool things with cool people and center other people in the narrative of my story that I felt deserving. Then, it allowed me to turn it right back to them and give more impactful work to the people in my audience.

It brought me a deeper connection with people who inspired me and allowed me to inspire more people.

I have always said that money is the byproduct of running a good business, not the reason for it.

To me, this is everything. We each have a finite number of collaborations we can do in a year, and I want mine to be as impactful as possible. I only have a finite number of launches every year, and I want those to be as impactful as possible.

If I do that, more people will be more deeply impacted by the work that moves them. Therefore, audience growth is in service of making those as impactful as possible.

Over 18,000 people open at least one email from me a week. That's more than the number of people who attend most conventions in this country. ***That is why I care about audience growth***, not so I get a higher number...but because I can impact more humans with the message I want to tell.

Money, for money's sake, is a terrible way to exist.

My intention every day is to meet cool people, commingle the smartest people I know, and allow good things to happen. The bigger my audience, the more power that network has, and the more power I have to help my friends and people I respect do cool projects and live their best life. I think about Brandon Sanderson's $41 million Kickstarter. It started with him dropping a surprise link into his massive Reddit community and allowing it to spider out from there.

Yes, he stoked the flames, but mainly, his audience carried the message, and let me tell you, those books are weird. ***They are so weird, and I love them***

so much. He was allowed to get weird with it and make life-changing money because he had an audience for his work already.

Money is a byproduct of having an audience, and money is nice, but what I want is the freedom that having a larger audience provides and the opportunities that come with that.

People who I have always admired and been inspired by are now part of my network. They are now excited to work with me on projects, and it's incredible. That is the power of having an audience. ***I am in service to that feeling.*** This kind of work is supposed to set you free, not yoke you down.

However, it is hard, and it's hard to see through the hard work. Even when this work is easy, it is hard, and it is rarely ever easy.

Living in capitalism is bad for your mental health. Art is a way to improve your mental health. Combining capitalism with your art links the thing you do to improve your mental health directly with the thing destroying it.

It takes a lot to separate the ***making*** of a thing from the ***making money*** on a thing.

What's the solution here beyond improving your mindset? It's probably diversifying your income streams beyond Substack into other areas, like Kickstarter, conventions, consulting, courses, etc. The more income streams you have working, the more stable you will feel. I've been doing this a long time, and I've never had the same income stream perform for me the same way in back-to-back years. It's only been from the diversity of my income that I've been able to keep my income consistent for the past several years. ***We are all looking for a magic bullet, but there are really only bullets, and each one can hurt as much as help.***

There's one question I think we should ask when we see so many shiny objects coming at us at once.

Will I do it, though?

Every single time you see something come along, the #1 way to know if it will help you move forward or burn you out is whether you will do it. If it's a perfect strategy, but you won't do it...then it's actually just a terrible distraction.

If it's awkward and clunky, but you'll actually do it without burning out...then you should do it.

...ooooh, did you notice how I added something there?

...without burning out.

Burning out means a lot of things, but what I mean by it is whether the effort you expend will more than replenish itself before your energy depletes.

That might be monetary, social, mental, or just about anything. You can train yourself to do more or different things, but right now, this minute, you might not have space for a thing, and need to create some, or not.

A candle will go on forever if you keep providing a wick for it to burn. It will burn twice as fast if you burn a candle on both ends.

There are so many things that I want to do but will never do, so I either hire for those things, plan how to make space for them, or move on from them. It literally doesn't matter if it's the greatest idea in the world. If you don't have space, can't make space, or don't want to make space for it, you should move on from it.

Productivity is really about doing fewer things that move you along more than it is doing things faster. Once you know what's for you, this whole game gets way easier.

It's messy, sloppy, and can get contentious when you ***literally*** put a price on your soul. That's why I wrote a book called *How to Build Your Creative Career.* What you might not know is the subtitle of that book is ***...without selling your soul.***

I have been doing this ***exact*** work for a long time. It is the work of a lifetime, and even then, it's almost impossible. It's not the best way to end a book, but that speaks to the mess of it all. It helps to be gentle with yourself and give a lot of grace to everyone as they try to work through it. ***I know that's what I'm gonna do.***

*

It's over! If you have questions, make sure to find Claire Venus at https://substack.com/@clairevenus and Russell at https://www.theauthorstack.com.

- -